Golden Years
of
West Bromwich

Part of the
Memories
series

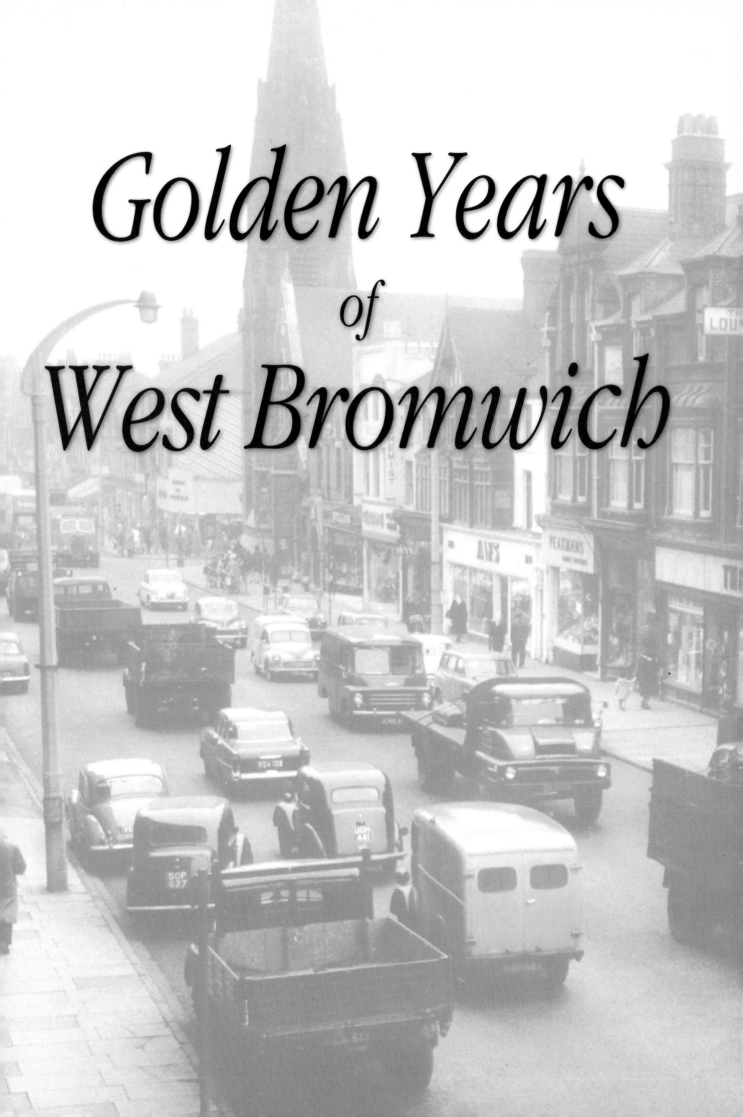

Golden Years
of
West Bromwich

*The Publishers would like to thank the following companies for supporting
the production of this book*

Main Sponsor

I.M. Group Limited

Adcocks Solicitors

Anglo Holt Construction Limited

Bromford Iron & Steel Company Limited

Fuller & Sons (Transport) Limited

WH Keys Limited

JH Lavender & Company Limited

Fred Smith & Sons (Motor Bodies) Limited

First published in Great Britain by True North Books Limited
Units 3 - 5 Heathfield Industrial Park
Elland West Yorkshire
HX5 9AE
Tel. 01422 377977
© Copyright: True North Books Limited 1999

ISBN 1 900463 99 7

Text, design and origination by True North Books Limited
Printed and bound by The Amadeus Press Limited

Memories are made of this

Memories. We all have them: people, places and events, some good and some bad. Our memories of the place where we grew up are usually tucked away in a very special place in our mind. The best are probably connected with our childhood and youth, when we longed to be grown up and paid no attention to adults who told us to enjoy being young, as these were the best years of our lives. We look back now and realise that they were right.

Old photographs bring our memories flooding back - coronations and celebrations; talking pictures, Technicolor and television; the war years, rationing, and the shared hopes and fears which created such a warm community spirit; buying things made of nylon and plastic; fashions which took trouser-bottoms and hemlines from drainpipes and mini-skirts to the other extreme; Doris Day, Acker Bilk, Elvis Presley and the Beatles; the jitterbug, the tango and discos; Ford Populars and Minis; decimalisation. Life changed so much over the years. Some changes were big, some small; some altered our lives in ways we never anticipated. Who in the early days of motoring could have foreseen the motorways and traffic systems of the latter decades of the 20th century? Did any of us realise, when we first saw a computer, what a tremendous impact they would have on our lives? Self-service supermarkets and frozen food made our lives easier - but at the expense of our friendly little corner shops. Nostalgia is always such a mixture of feelings . . . We hope that the collection of pictures in this book will remind you of happy days in bygone eras - and who knows, you might even have been there when one of the photographs was taken!

Contents

Section one

Events & occasions

•

Section two

On the move

•

Section three

Around the town centre

•

Section four

On the home front

•

Section five

Shopping spree

•

Section six

At work

West Bromwich through the years

Nobody who has grown up in the Black Country needs to be told what a marvellous place it is to live in - full of warm-hearted people with their own brand of irrepressible humour. Traditionally the home of the iron and steel industry, the area cannot be said to have had an easy passage through the 20th century, with its catalogue of trade recessions and competition from other sources.

But West Bromwich, home of so many great British firms, can be proud of its continued success and development throughout this period. Golden Years of West Bromwich is a collection of photographs which we hope will stir memories for everybody who grew up within its boundaries. Here you will find snapshots of everyday life in times gone by - the town centre as it used to be before we ever even dreamed of shopping precincts and pedestrian zones, the trams, buses and trains we used to catch, the schools we attended, the firms where we worked and the much-needed new housing estates which were built for us to live in after the second world war. And you will also find pictures of some of those special events and occasions which are the subject of so many happy childhood memories - the street parties with which we in West Bromwich celebrated the coronations of King George VI and of Queen Elizabeth II, the 1951 Festival of Britain, the Trade Fairs, carnivals, Royal occasions . . . and much more. Readers who were there at the time may well recognise themselves in the pages of this book - while younger readers seeing these photographs for the first time will, we hope, be interested to see how the town where their parents and grandparents grew up developed into the West Bromwich of today.

Events & occasions

Below: How many hours of practice went into perfecting this impressive display, we wonder - and how many bruised shins, banged elbows and embarrassing moments were endured along the way? These dozen intrepid gymnasts and their brave teacher were photographed for posterity in the grounds of Wigmore School, as it was then. Construction of this building, an imposing landmark over the Newton valley, was begun in 1870 and it was opened two years later as a boarding school for children from the local workhouses. It is clear from the favourable accounts placed on record by former pupils in later years that the school went on to develop into a thriving community, and provided many children with a good start in life which they would not otherwise have had. However, by the 1930s pupil numbers were falling, and in 1936 it became a Home Office Approved School. Shortly after the war it switched its attentions to the other end of the age range, becoming instead offices for the Ministry of Pensions, and in 1964 was taken over by West Bromwich Corporation.

Right: Edward, Prince of Wales, was a popular figure; his infectious smile and his charming manners won the hearts of the whole nation, and when he visited West Bromwich on Wednesday 13th June 1923 the town turned it into a day of celebration. All municipal employees who were not actually involved in the proceedings were given a half day holiday on full pay, and after the Prince had departed festivities continued in the Park in the form of a musical evening. Dartmouth Park had in fact been central to the Prince of Wales' visit, as he had formally presented the freehold of the Park, which was opened in 1878, to the Mayor. However, perhaps the most touching moment of his visit came when, after inspecting a parade of members of British Legion and Ex-Servicemen, the Prince met an assembly of disabled soldiers and the orphans and widows of those killed in the war. A glance at the faces of those shown in this photograph shows the effect of HRH Prince Edward's kind words upon the brave men who had suffered for their country: their eyes are riveted on him, gleaming with pride. A moment to remember, indeed, and no doubt one which stayed with them for the rest of their lives. On a less solemn note, the Prince was presented with a silver-mounted hunting crop by the schoolchildren of the borough - and in return, he gave them the best present any schoolchild can have: a day's holiday, to be taken on the Friday after his visit!

There is a striking absence of flags, bunting and cheering crowds to mark this royal visit, and the date of the photograph tells us why: 19th April 1940. King George VI and Queen Elizabeth are seen here leaving West Bromwich railway station, accompanied by Lord Dudley, Regional Commissioner for Civil Defence, Councillor Edward Woodward, Mayor, and Mr G F Dallow, Town Clerk. During the second world war members of the Royal family did all they could to help keep up morale, sending messages to badly-affected districts and visiting towns and cities throughout the country. The nation appreciated this genuine display of concern; after all, the Royal family could have shut themselves off somewhere safe for the duration of the war, had they wished, but instead they chose to share the plight of the nation. However, their movements were kept as secret as possible for security reasons; their visits received no advance publicity, and the only crowds that gathered were generally composed of people who had been going about their daily business, happened to notice that something out of the ordinary was going on and out of curiosity had loitered to watch.

Above: Preparations for celebrating the coronation of Elizabeth II kept practically the whole of West Bromwich busy for months before the big day. As well as the official programme of events organised by the Council and other organisations, countless Coronation funds were set up by local shopkeepers and groups of neighbours who bravely took upon themselves the mammoth task of organising street parties for the resident youngsters. Everybody who wanted to be included would donate money or goodies - some collections raised as much as £400 - and when the day arrived, tables groaned beneath the weight of sandwiches, jellies and blancmanges. Often there were paper hats, and sometimes trumpets and squeakers were provided to get the party spirit going - though it is not recorded whether the organisers ever regretted their generosity later on when their eardrums began to ring - and any money left over was spent on buying souvenir mugs, sweets and suchlike for the little ones, and plaques or other commemorative items for couples without

children who had contributed to the fund. Here we see the ladies of Union Street taking a breather in between setting out the table and giving the signal for the feasting to start. Readers who went to a Coronation Day party in June 1953 probably never stopped to think of all the hard work and preparation that had gone into it, but the grown-ups did not expect gratitude. Happy smiles were thanks enough.

Top: We are in the throes of General Election fever, 1929; the crowd is marching through Rydding Square, and the man they all support can be seen towards the left of the picture, wearing a white shirt and bow tie. He's the Right Honourable F O Roberts, West Bromwich's Labour MP ever since 1918. This year his opponents are Mr W Ramage, the Liberal candidate, and Conservative candidate Captain J I Chesshire, and since Monday, 8th April Mr Roberts has been campaigning hard on issues such as unemployment, housing and trade - some things never change! Unemployment was a particularly sensitive issue at the time, and was to become even more so during the 30s with queues at the Labour Exchanges all over the country reaching an unprecedented length. However, although the Government had not found the answer to that problem, it had addressed the housing shortage by introducing a number of incentives to spur on the house building programme, and its efforts were appreciated in West Bromwich where there was widespread concern over housing. Mr Roberts had a great deal of support - as we can see - and confidently expected to keep his seat; which he did, and with a comfortable majority. On polling day 19,621 of the West Bromwich electorate voted Labour, and the Conservatives came second with 10,943 votes. With the exception of the period between 1931 and 1935, Mr Roberts was to remain MP for West Bromwich until 1941.

Events of the 1930s

HOT OFF THE PRESS
The years of the 1930s saw Adolf Hitler's sickening anti-Jewish campaign echoed in the streets of Britain. On 19th October 1936 Oswald Mosley's 7,000-strong British Union of Fascists clashed head on with thousands of Jews and Communists in London, resulting in 80 people being injured in the ensuing battle. Mosley and his 'blackshirts' later rampaged through the streets beating up Jews and smashing the windows of their businesses.

GETTING AROUND
At the beginning of the decade many believed that the airship was the transport of the future. The R101 airship, however, loaded with thousands of cubic metres of hydrogen, crashed in France on its maiden flight in 1930. Forty-eight passengers and crew lost their lives. In 1937 the Hindenburg burst into flames - the entire disaster caught on camera and described by a distraught reporter. The days of the airship were numbered.

SPORTING CHANCE
In 1939 British racing driver Sir Malcolm Campbell hit the headlines when he captured the world's water-speed record for the third time in 'Bluebird' - all his cars were given the same name. A racing driver who set world speed records both on land and on water, Sir Malcolm established world land-speed records no fewer than nine times. His son Donald went on to set further records, tragically dying in 1967 when his speedboat - also named 'Bluebird' - crashed.

These charming young ladies were pupils of Cronehills Central School somewhere around 1930; where are they all now, we wonder, and are any of them reading this book? Cronehills Central opened in 1925, subsequently taking on the role of Secondary Technical School. In fact, initial moves to set it up had begun before the first world war, with the site being

identified as early as 1912. If West Bromwich was in need of a new elementary school in 1912, its needs were far greater by the time the plan came to fruition - as we can see from the size of this class, numbering 46 pupils in total. Alderman Sir George Kenrick was invited to give an address at the opening ceremony, and the town was delighted when he accepted; in return, Sir George had the pleasure and privilege of hearing the school choir singing 'Rolling Down To Rio', rehearsed specially for the occasion - well worth a trip to West Bromwich!

This page: In 1939 Britain's Prime Minister Neville Chamberlain had made his announcement to the waiting people of Britain that '...this country is at war with Germany.' The country rolled up its sleeves and prepared for the inevitable. This war would be different from other wars. This time planes had the ability to fly further and carry a heavier load, and air raids were fully expected. Air raid shelters were obviously going to be needed, and shelters were built on open places across the town.

By the time war was declared an army of volunteers of both sexes had already been recruited to form an Air Raid Protection service. At first ARP personnel were unpaid volunteers but when war broke out in September 1939 they became paid staff. It was their job to patrol specified areas, making sure that no chinks of light broke the blackout restrictions, checking the safety of local residents, being alert for gas attacks, air raids and unexploded bombs. The exceptional work done by Air Raid Wardens in dealing with incendiaries, giving first aid to the injured, helping to rescue victims from their bombed-out properties, clearing away rubble, and a thousand and one other tasks became legendary; during the second world war nearly as many private citizens were killed as troops - and many of them were the gallant ARP wardens.

Other preparations were hastily made around the town. Place names and other identifying marks were obliterated to confuse the enemy about exactly where they were. Notices went up everywhere giving good advice to citizens on a number of issues. 'Keep Mum - she's not so dumb' warned people to take care what kind of information they passed on, as the person they were speaking to could be an enemy. Older readers will remember how difficult it was to find certain items in the shops during the war; combs, soap, cosmetics, hairgrips, elastic, buttons, zips - all were virtually impossible to buy as factories that once produced these items had been turned over to war work. Stockings were in short supply, and resourceful women resorted to colouring their legs with gravy browning or with a mixture of sand and water. Beetroot juice was found to be a good substitute for lipstick. Clothes rationing was introduced in 1941, and everyone had 66 coupons per year. Eleven coupons would buy a dress, and sixteen were needed for a coat. The number of coupons was later reduced to 40 per person. People were required to save material where they could - ladies' hemlines went up considerably, and skirts were not allowed to have lots of pleats. Some found clever ways around the regulations by using materials that were not rationed. Blackout material could be embroidered and made into blouses or skirts, and dyed sugar sacks were turned into curtains.

Above: War had been declared, and every citizen of Britain, young and old, male and female, was called upon to put his or her back into the war effort. Those who did not go into military service of one kind or another worked in factories, dug for victory, gave up their aluminium baths and saucepans, joined organisations and aided in any way they could. These boys were not going to be left out; they might be too young to fight but while there were sandbags to be filled they were going to do their bit to protect their school building. Thousands of sandbags were used during World War II to protect the country and its beautiful civic buildings.

Left: A proud father poses for the camera with his latest arrival. The baby had not arrived from Mars, in fact the 'arrival' was not a baby at all, but an anti-gas attack suit which was compulsory for babies in the United Kingdom during the second world war. An air pump at the side of the suit enabled anxious parents to replenish the supply of air to the precious package inside. It is said that most babies were less than enthusiastic abut the prospect of being encased in the suit - and who could blame them? The picture was taken in 1939. In the event there was never any gas attack on British soil during the course of the second world war.

It was too bad of the weather not to rise to the occasion on the day George VI was crowned King - but West Bromwich had made up its mind to celebrate, so celebrate it did. Even the sports in the Park went ahead in spite of the rain. Festivities were planned for every day of the week - which was not the case in all towns - and everyone agreed that the borough's week of revelry was the most fun they had ever had. The traders had clubbed together to buy electric lights and other decorations, and the council had organised all manner of splendid events which included the firing of a 31-gun salute at Dartmouth Park and various parades and processions. Saturday night's grand finale took the form of a firework display featuring portraits of the King and Queen, followed by a torchlit procession through the streets to the Town Hall. During the week the Town Hall had been the venue for the Pageant of Empire, which went down extremely well. Among the week's civic occasions were the opening of the new St John Ambulance Brigade Headquarters at Oakwood, and the opening of a children's playground at Carlsbrooke Road, Friar Park - where much to everybody's amusement the youngsters did not even wait for the opening ceremony to finish before getting stuck in! There were Coronation gifts for all the children of the Borough - a new penny, an orange, a decorated pencil, a Coronation mug - while for many kiddies the best part of all was getting their knees under the table and making sure they ate at least their fair share of sandwiches and jelly. This photograph tells us that the street party in Glover Street was pretty popular with the grown-ups too!

Events of the 1930s

MELODY MAKERS

Throughout the 1930s a young American trombonist called Glenn Miller was making his mark in the world of music. By 1939 the Glenn Miller sound was a clear leader in the field; his clean-cut, meticulously executed arrangements of numbers such as 'A String of Pearls' and 'Moonlight Serenade' brought him fame across the world as a big-band leader. During a flight to England from Paris in 1944 Miller's plane disappeared; no wreckage was ever found.

THE WORLD AT LARGE

In India, Gandhi's peaceful protests against British rule were gathering momentum. The Salt Laws were a great bone of contention: forced to buy salt from the British government, thousands of protestors marched to the salt works, intending to take it over in the name of the Indian people. Policemen and guards attacked the marchers, but not one of them fought back. Gandhi, who earned for himself the name 'Mahatma' - Great Soul - was assassinated in 1948.

INVENTION AND TECHNOLOGY

With no driving tests or speed restrictions, 120,000 people were killed on the roads in Britain between the two world wars. In 1934 Percy Shaw invented a safety device destined to become familiar the world over: reflecting roadstuds. In dark or foggy conditions the studs that reflected light from the car's headlights kept traffic on the 'straight and narrow' and must over the years have saved many lives.

In 1930 West Bromwich District Hospital decided to try a new way of raising funds: it would hold a Carnival. Hoping for good weather, the Committee chose the week 20th to 27th September and set about deciding what events to include. A Carnival Queen was an absolute must; and then there would be processions and bands, competitions, roasts, and fireworks. Gradually their plans took shape. The opening procession would set off from the Town Hall make its way to Dartmouth Park, headed by the West Bromwich Excelsior Silver Band, and with a Jester and a Pirate King to lead the festivities. In the Park, Miss May Hodgetts would be crowned

Carnival Queen. Competitions would include general exhibits, tableaux, collections, jazz bands, sports and fancy dress for both adults and children. There would be a motor-cycle rodeo. There would be a confetti battle. In fact there would be something for everyone. The only thing the Committee could not guarantee was the weather, and sure enough it poured down on the first day - but the Carnival went on regardless: Queen May was crowned in the Town Hall instead and nipped out to wave to the crowd in a convenient sunny interval, and some sports were able to take place although others were abandoned. Literally dozens of jazz bands turned up, and the sheep and ox-roasts were a tremendous success, with sandwiches being auctioned off and attracting plenty of bidders. So, although no doubt more people would have joined in the first day's processions and thrown their coppers into the collectors' tins if the sun had been shining, the organisers' efforts had by no means been in vain.

This stunning fancy dress parade has filled Tyndal Street with a marvellous collections of characters - Red Indians in grass skirts, a multitude of queens in ermines and crowns, patriotically-attired children, a Charlie Chaplain - and somewhere in the crowd, if the placard raised aloft is to be believed, is A British Onion - what a shame we can't see him (or her)! The parade was part of the festivities with which West Bromwich celebrated the coronation of Her Majesty Queen Elizabeth II. No doubt this location appealed to the photographer because of

its impressive street decorations, including the wonderful crown above the heads of the parade. In fact Tyndal Street was judged the best decorated street in West Bromwich at the time of the Coronation, and a cash prize was presented to the street by Councillor Mrs Ruth Parfitt.

There were so many beautifully-decorated streets that while the judges must have thoroughly enjoyed the task of touring round and inspecting them, actually coming to a decision must have been extremely difficult. But Tyndal Street won, and the second prize went to Chapel Street.

The King is dead, long live the Queen! King George VI's death on 6th February 1952 was followed by the Proclamation of Accession of Queen Elizabeth II. A crowd of some 500 assembled in front of West Bromwich Town Hall to hear the Proclamation being read by the Mayor, Alderman Arthur Medley. In spite of the haste with which the occasion had been organised, it was an impressive ceremony, with the approach of the Mayoral procession, with the Mayor attired in full regalia, greeted by a fanfare from the Buglers of the Sea Cadets. The subdued crowd, in deep mourning for their late beloved King, listened solemnly and took some consolation from the Mayor's concluding words, 'God save the Queen'.

The nation already had a great affection for the pretty young Princess Elizabeth, who, in training for the accession from a very early age, had carried out her public duties admirably. The mixed emotions of the people were reflected in the confusion which arose over flags. Although it was widely assumed that these should fly at half mast following the death of the King, they should in fact have been at the masthead from sunrise to sunset on Proclamation Day.

Events of the 1930s

SCIENCE AND DISCOVERY
By observing the heavens, astronomers had long believed that there in the constellation of Gemini lay a new planet, so far undiscovered. They began to search for the elusive planet, and a special astronomical camera was built for the purpose. The planet Pluto was discovered by amateur astronomer Clyde Tombaugh in 1930, less than a year later.

WHAT'S ON?
In this heyday of the cinema, horrified audiences were left gasping at the sight of Fay Wray in the clutches of the giant ape in the film 'King Kong', released in 1933. Very different but just as gripping was the gutsy 1939 American Civil War romance 'Gone with the Wind'. Gable's parting words, 'Frankly, my dear, I don't give a damn' went down in history.

ROYAL WATCH
The talking point of the early 1930s was the affair of the Prince of Wales, who later became King Edward VIII, and American divorcee Wallis Simpson. Faced with a choice, Edward gave up his throne for 'the woman I love' and spent the remainder of his life in exile. Many supported him, though they might not have been as keen to do so if they had been aware of his Nazi sympathies, kept strictly under wraps at the time.

Above: Coronation Day, 1953, did not enjoy the best of weather, but that did not stop everyone enjoying themselves. The official programme included both indoor and outdoor events. There was plenty happening in Dartmouth Park - band concerts on Monday, Wednesday and Saturday, open air dancing on Tuesday, Wednesday and Saturday, sports and keep fit displays on Wednesday, and an ox roast and a firework display on Saturday; while events inside the Town Hall included a civic service on Monday, and a televised viewing of the ceremony itself on Coronation Day. This was many people's first experience of television, and all over the country we gazed at our small, flickery, black-and-white screens, totally enthralled by this miracle of technology that allowed us to witness such a great event as it took place. All over the borough special events were arranged, many of them for children; on this photograph we see all the children who have turned up to the Rex cinema, Hill Top. The cinema was hired by Mr A Edwards for two days to give special film shows for children, and you can't go far wrong with a good Western. Dallas (1950) starred Gary Cooper, while Flowing Gold (1940) featured John Garfield and Pat O'Brien.

Right: The sooner everybody present stops kicking each other under the table, faces the camera and smiles, the sooner the photographer will be able to stand down and the yard of Old Cottage Spring public house in Crookhay Lane will be filled with shrill, excited voices and the clattering of crockery. Just look at those plates piled high with sandwiches, and the waiting dishes of trifle and fruit! As usual the grown-ups are fussing about things that don't matter, and to humour them the mites are patiently saying cheese and trying to curb their impatience to get down to the real business of the day. But we have to admit perhaps the grown-ups were right for once, as posterity would have been the poorer without this charming snapshot. And they will not have to wait for long now. Once the photographer is satisfied, the word will be given, and then the sandwiches will disappear in next to no time, the trifle will follow, the party hats will slip over one eye, and the best clothes will no longer look quite so smart after a few close encounters with sandwich filling and jelly. The food stains will wash out, but the happy memories of this Coronation Day party, and of similar ones all over West Bromwich, will stay with these children for the rest of their lives.

Above: You'd be hard pressed to recognise this omnibus as the property of West Bromwich Corporation, illuminated as it is by more than 1,000 lights - powered by 60 ten-volt batteries - and decorated with scenes depicting the development of road passenger transport in West Bromwich over the preceding 100 years. The 1951 Festival of Britain, held on the centenary of the original 1851 Festival, was a celebration of British industry, and was intended to inspire the nation with a spirit of optimism, helping them put the difficulties of the war years behind them and face the future with confidence. So

colourful, extravagant displays were the order of the day, and West Bromwich certainly came up with the goods. Streets were decorated, the borough's new Garden of Remembrance was floodlit by green, red and white lights, and the town turned into a blaze of light and colour, day and night. This exquisite bus - decorated along similar lines to the one which marked the 1939 Coronation - was an important feature of the celebrations.

Below: This is the town model which went on display early in 1965, finally putting an end to months, even years of intense speculation on what the future held for the centre of West Bromwich. In fact, rumours had begun circulating as early as 1959, spiced up by the occasional 'leak' of information. It was generally agreed that radical redevelopment was necessary to improve central facilities and to avoid business decay, and by 1963 the Council had made a great deal of progress with its plans for improvements in the spheres of housing, education and social services, as well as in town centre redevelopment. However, the official unveiling of this model provoked fierce opposition from some quarters, and a certain amount of political bickering ensued. A major cause of dissatisfaction appears to have been the Council's alleged lack of prior consultation with the Chamber of Trade. Difficulties caused by the plans themselves seem to have been mainly centred around fears that rates would increase, and that the fringe traders would suffer.

On the move

'Try Typhoo tea for indigestion', the advertisement on tram number 558 suggests; whether or not this would pass muster with today's Advertising Standards Authority is a moot point. After all, they're only inviting you to try it - they don't say that it will work! Advertisers did not lose their space when West Brom lost its trams, as omnibuses took over the secondary role of mobile advertisement hoarding along with the primary role of people-carrier in 1939. Although many people missed trams when they went, West Bromwich's cyclists were not among them; anyone who has ever got their front wheel stuck in a tramline will know what a menace that could be - especially if a tram happened to be bearing down on you at the time! The overhead carriers disappeared very soon after the trams themselves, and the tracks were not long in following - all except for a few feet of tramline in Crowthers Yard, off Paradise Street, which somehow managed to remain in situ.

In 1956 the clip-clop of horses' hooves was still to be heard on the streets of West Bromwich - this particular horse obviously does not think that the No Waiting sign applies to him - and nobody got offended by term like 'old age pensioners'. In these more enlightened days it has occurred to us that calling old people old is not polite, so after struggling with various euphemisms - OAP was popular for a long time - we finally settled upon Senior Citizen. Political correctness has spread to other walks of life too, and most of us must have been shocked to discover how insensitive we had been all our lives without even realising it. Today's youngsters

Events of the 1940s

WHAT'S ON?
In wartime Britain few families were without a wireless set. It was the most popular form of entertainment, and programmes such as ITMA, Music While You Work and Workers' Playtime provided the people with an escape from the harsh realities of bombing raids and ration books. In 1946 the BBC introduced the Light Programme, the Home Service and the Third Programme, which gave audiences a wider choice of listening.

GETTING AROUND
October 1948 saw the production of Britain's first new car designs since before the war. The Morris Minor was destined for fame as one of the most popular family cars, while the four-wheel-drive Land Rover answered the need for a British-made off-road vehicle. The country was deeply in the red, however, because of overseas debts incurred during the war. The post-war export drive that followed meant that British drivers had a long wait for their own new car.

SPORTING CHANCE
American World Heavyweight Boxing Champion Joe Louis, who first took the title back in 1937, ruled the world of boxing during the 1930s and 40s, making a name for himself as unbeatable. Time after time he successfully defended his title against all comers, finally retiring in 1948 after fighting an amazing 25 title bouts throughout his boxing career. Louis died in 1981 at the age of 67.

who have grown up with the politically correct terminology are never tempted to call a chalkboard anything other than a chalkboard, but those of us who are older sometimes find it difficult to remember the new vocabulary. However, in 1956 pensioners were apparently less coy about admitting their age - especially if being old meant they could get in to a special Monday night show!

Above: Vacuum packs, freeze-dried packs, ingeniously-designed packets that you can't get into - we may think of packaging as a modern obsession, but clearly it already in the public eye by 1957, with Elkes Biscuits very eager to let everybody know about their sealed air-tight packets. Even those of us with Green leanings, who feel that far too many of the world's valuable resources end up in our kitchen waste bin, will have to agree that biscuits are greatly improved by proper packaging that keeps them fresh and crisp. Anyone who remembers the days when you bought biscuits out of a tin at the local grocer's will remember how soft they used to get; if you happened to buy them when the shopkeeper had recently opened a new tin you were all right, but if you were unlucky enough to get the last half pound out of a tin that had been open for several days, they would be distinctly soggy. And someone had to buy the last biscuits in the tin!

Above right: This scene might be depressingly familiar to any readers who were unfortunate enough to find themselves out of work around the time this photograph was taken in 1956: the Employment Exchange in Paradise Street. At least by this time the post-war state welfare system was in place, thanks to far-reaching legislation worked out by William Beveridge. The system of national insurance cards and contributions stamps for workers had been intro-duced by the National Insurance Act of 1946. Until 1961 contributions were paid at a flat rate. The National Insurance Act had also given responsibility for social security payments to the newly-established Ministry of National Insurance, in Newcastle, and instituted the dual practice of paying sickness and unemployment benefits through the Employment Exchange and old age pensions through the Post Office. It was not until 1961 that graduated insurance contributions were introduced, on the basis that the more we earned, the more we paid in, and - in theory, at least - the better the pension we could look forward to when we retired.

Right: Buses took over from trams in 1939, but they had been around on the streets of West Bromwich before then, and in fact this photograph of bus number 17, registration number EA 7575, indicates that it entered service on 10th April 1936. In these perhaps more cynical days, the first thing we ask when innovation or change is announced is, 'How much will it cost?' The introduction of the omnibus in 1939 cost the good people of West Bromwich nothing at all, in terms of fare increases; West Bromwich was one of a small number of boroughs which made had made a long-term undertaking not to increase its fares, so that in fact a journey on one of the new motorbuses in 1939 would have cost you not a farthing more than the same journey would have cost in 1914.

Below: How many unmarried bus passengers used to gaze longingly into the window of Alberta's of Birmingham and dream about their wedding day as they passed this spot each day! The bridal industry had enjoyed an exceptionally busy period all over the country some five years prior to this photograph, which was taken in 1952. Many an engaged couple had decided to wait until after the war to tie the knot, making 1946 and 1947 boom years for weddings - although with a waiting-list for houses of well over 5,000 people in 1946, it was an anxious time for West Bromwich couples wanting to set up just then. However, the Corporation pulled out all the stops and by 1958 it had completed 5,557 properties, while private developers were also busy and young people were being encouraged to take out mortgages and buy their own houses. Another knock-on effect of the sudden flood of marriages was a sharp increase in the birth rate in Britain. The post-war baby boom or 'bulge' peaked around 1950, and this in turn led to pressure on schools when class sizes increased over the following decades; so the social repercussions of World War II were to be much longer-lasting than many people had anticipated.

Events of the 1940s

HOT OFF THE PRESS

At the end of World War II in 1945 the Allies had their first sight of the unspeakable horrors of the Nazi extermination camps they had only heard of until then. In January, 4,000 emaciated prisoners more dead than alive were liberated by the Russians from Auschwitz in Poland, where three million people, most of them Jews,were murdered. The following year 23 prominent Nazis faced justice at Nuremberg; 12 of them were sentenced to death for crimes against humanity.

THE WORLD AT LARGE

The desert area of Alamogordo in New Mexico was the scene of the first atomic bomb detonation on July 16, 1945. With an explosive power equal to more than 15,000 tons of TNT, the flash could be seen 180 miles away. President Truman judged that the bomb could secure victory over Japan with far less loss of US lives than a conventional invasion, and on 6th August the first of the new weapons was dropped on Hiroshima. Around 80,000 people died.

ROYAL WATCH

By the end of World War II, the 19-year-old Princess Elizabeth and her distant cousin Lieutenant Philip Mountbatten RN were already in love. The King and Queen approved of Elizabeth's choice of husband, though they realised that she was rather young and had not mixed with many other young men. The engagement announcement was postponed until the Princess had spent four months on tour in Africa. The couple's wedding on 20th November 1947 was a glittering occasion - the first royal pageantry since before the war.

Try driving a bus the full length of Paradise Street today, and see how far you get . . . Younger readers - and even older ones - may well reply, 'Where's Paradise Street?' In fact the two ends are still there, though the middle stretch has disappeared beneath the Sandwell Centre, and as a street it no longer has any coherent identity. The 19th century gables which used to

be such a familiar sight to passengers on the top deck of the number 25 to Sutton have long gone. Sutton Coldfield, of course, has been a favourite place for a day out for families from Birmingham and the surrounding towns; many generations will have fond memories of packing their picnic hampers, boarding the bus, and keeping their fingers crossed that the sun stays out for their little expedition to their favourite spot. Although from time to time there has been talk of building on Sutton Coldfield's extensive parkland, fortunately this has never happened.

Above: This single decker, No 106, pictured here in August 1957, was one of the minority of West Bromwich Corporation buses which were fitted with a Jensen body. During all-too-brief period of success which came to an end in 1976, Jensen, most famous for its fibre-glass bodied Interceptor, was based not far from Carters Green. This particular bus entered service in March 1940 and was withdrawn in June 1961; on this occasion it looks rather as though its entire consignment of passengers has been lured away by Burton's special offer of ready to wear slacks. Montague Burton's good quality menswear has been a firm favourite with the gentlemen for many generations, and the chain grew until virtually every town and city in Britain had at least one branch. The story goes that when soldiers were demobbed after military service they were given vouchers to be fitted out in civvies at Burton's. They went along to the nearest branch and were kitted out in what was then termed 'the full Monty' - and that is the origin of the phrase which has in recent years come to mean something very different from a full suit of clothes!

Above right: All lined up on the starting grid and ready to leap into action to convey the people of West Bromwich safely to their destinations: this batch of buses was part of the original tramway replacement fleet, pictured here at the Oak Lane depot in March 1939. Omnibus enthusiasts will no doubt recognise the technical configuration of the fleet - Metro-Cammell-Weymann bodies, Daimler COG6 chassis - and also the unusual position of the headlights, much lower than most bus fleets. During the war, the tips of the mudguards were picked out in white as a safety measure to make the buses visible to other road users in blackout conditions. People's ears, attuned to picking out the clickety-clack of approaching trams, now had to learn instead to distinguish the rumbling notes of the bus engines from the other traffic sounds.

This is the West Bromwich Corporation omnibus fleet, pictured at the Oak Lane depot in 1952. The headlights are higher than those on the original 1930s fleet, and the single front spotlight on the kerbside, a feature of older buses, would be angled so as to pick out the edge of the pavement in the thick pea-soup fogs which, thankfully, we no longer seem to experience. The open back gave passengers much more leeway when it came to getting on and off the bus; the athletes among us could give chase and leap on as it pulled away from a stop, or if you came across your bus stuck in traffic between stops you could hop on there and then rather than walk along to the next stop and wait for it, or equally you could jump off at the corner of your own street rather than at the official bus stop. You weren't supposed to, of course, but the convenience made it well worth risking a brusque rebuke from a safety-conscious bus conductor. Bus conductors and conductresses varied in how strict they were about the number of standing passengers, too; with no door to close, the conductors had to put their foot down very firmly indeed to prevent passengers continuing to pile onto the platform even when the bus was officially full. Sailing along hanging out of the back, holding onto the rail and watching the road rush past, was actually a very exhilarating, if precarious, experience!

Traffic chaos around the junction of New Street and High Street used to be a common enough sight. This scene was captured for posterity in 1960; a traffic survey carried out that summer calculated an average daily flow of 650 vehicles per hour travelling in each direction along High Street, doubling to 1,300 during peak hours. And to add insult to injury, half of them didn't even want to be there; a survey of driver destinations revealed that 51 per cent was in fact through traffic and had no business in the town centre at all. The solution, of course, was to build an expressway to take traffic round, rather than through, the middle of West Bromwich; and so the West Bromwich Ringway

came into being. All the buildings to the right of the Star and Garter came down to make way for the dual carriageway that would turn scenes such as this one into a thing of the past, and allow the old Golden Mile to be turned over to the pedestrians. It seemed an ambitious plan when it was first announced, and some motorists grumbled about how much further they would have to drive to get from A to B, but it was not long before they realised that it was in fact much quicker, safer, and easier on the nerves than having to contend with this motley collection of trucks, vans, buses, lorries, with the odd jay-walking pedestrian thrown in for good measure!

Bottom: This type of bus was often referred to as the 'Daimler half-cab', though quite why the term should have become attached to this type in particular is something of a mystery as plenty of other buses had half cabs too. Bus 248 NEA entered service in 1963 and was captured on film in June 1969; the Daimler half-cab had a good reputation for giving reliable service, needing little maintenance and hardly ever coming up with a problem. Mature readers will know what the rectangular contraption in the centre above the upstairs windows was for: it was a ventilator, which let in fresh air when you opened it. Alternatively it was something for schoolchildren to play with and argue over when they had taken over the front seats and had begun getting bored on the journey home. Going upstairs on the bus had a couple of advantages when you were at school: first, the driver and conductor couldn't see what you were up to, and second, in the days when smoking was allowed on the upper deck only, the upstairs passengers were likely to be less prim and proper than the downstairs passengers, and so less likely to complain about your antics. It also gave you a cast-iron excuse for smelling of cigarette smoke, when your parents sniffed at your hair and clothes and accused you of smoking!

Right: A Number 74 is seen here on High Street in the August sunshine of 1952. In the background is the long-established High Street tailor Loo Bloom; between the wars L B Tailoring had been advertising suits right across the price range, from fifty bob (£2.50)

right up to five guineas (£5.25). And standing outside Loo Bloom's was a phenomenon that had existed since 1939: a woman bus conductress. After the initial surprise, passengers soon got used to women clippies and discovered that their quick repartee spiced with sharp Black Country humour could brighten up a journey to and from the daily grind. As the second world war progressed, women began to take on all kinds of jobs that had previously been looked upon as 'man's work', learning new skills and doing heavy, dirty tasks to keep the wheels of industry turning while the men were away at the front. Many women were reluctant to give up this new-found independence even when the men came back. The working woman was here to stay.

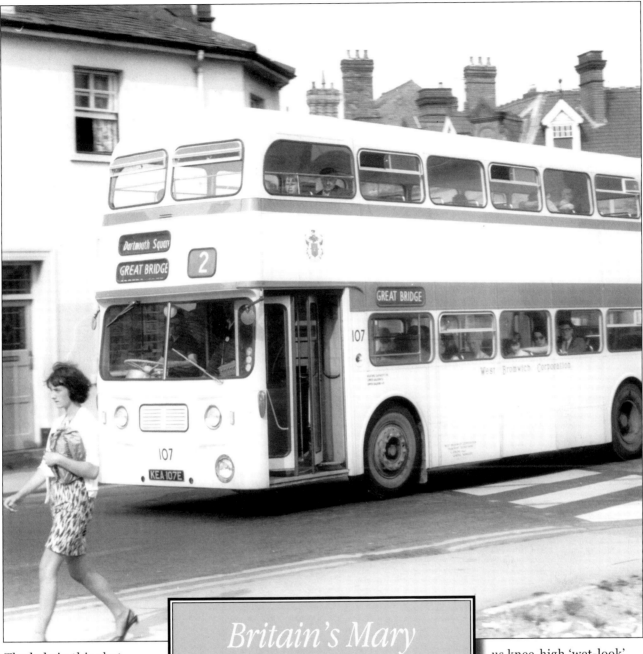

Britain's Mary Quant made her mark in the fashion industry in the 60s, earning herself an OBE in 1966

The lady in this shot leaves us in no doubt about the decade: short skirts, wicker baskets, white cardigans and sling-back shoes - it just has to be the 60s. The year of the photograph is in fact 1969. The hemline is not as extreme as some that shocked and outraged the older generation during the course of the swinging 60s. Comments made by fathers to teenage daughters varied according to how square or how tolerant the father in question was, and might range from a droll 'Aren't you going to put a skirt on?' to a brusque 'You're not going out looking like that!' As well as mini-skirts, the decade had brought us knee-high 'wet-look' boots, and Britain's Mary Quant had made her mark on the international fashion scene, earning herself an OBE in 1966. In part, it was the new man-made fibres which made these fashions possible; nylon tights allowed hemlines to rise without exposing unsightly stocking tops and suspenders, and the 'wet-look' was possible courtesy of the invention of stretch vinyl. By the end of the 60s, however, midis and maxis were also hitting the hemlines - much to the relief of those of us whose legs were, quite frankly, not made to wear minis!

Below: By 27th May 1957 the days of the steam locomotive were numbered, but this one is still doing a sterling job, pulling a train of iron ore wagons on behalf of Stewarts & Lloyds of Bilston. Watching the goods trains flashing past had a fascination all its own, even for non-trainspotters; you could try to read the writing on the sides of the trucks, or you could count the wagons (if it was not going too fast) in the hopes that it would turn out to be a particularly long one, so that you could boast about it later. And the purposeful pounding of hundreds of steel wheels conveyed a very reassuring message about the healthy state of British industry. Eddie-spotting is all very well in its way, but somehow there just isn't the same satisfaction in sitting on the M6 surrounded by heavy artics, and passing the time until the traffic starts to move again in reading the foreign names and website addresses on the sides of the trailers . . .

Right: The diesel railcar seen here at West Bromwich railway station is in fact the 11.15 am train from Dudley to Birmingham. Dudley and railways never really got on; after much customer dissatisfaction and complaints about the condition of the station and the service - Dudley was served by both the GWR and the LNWR - Dudley station closed in 1964. This photograph was in fact taken on 3rd May 1958, by which time the British Rail Modernisation Programme, which decreed that the future of rail travel lay in diesels and not in steam, was well underway and diesels were becoming an increasingly common sight. Although they were cleaner and quieter, once the novelty value had worn off many people came to the conclusion that they lacked character. Five years after this picture was taken, the GWR Carriage Works in Swindon, where so many great steam locomotives had been built over a period of almost a century, was to close - a sad day for steam buffs everywhere.

Above: Looking at this photograph, you can almost smell the cloud of steam . . . Anyone leaning out of the window of the Cambrian Coast Express may well be about to get a few smuts in their eyes as the Bristol Castle lets off steam, coasting down from West Bromwich to Swan Village. Wise people did not wear their best light-coloured coats to travel by steam train; it wasn't that the trains were dirty, but inevitably black bits came in through the open windows and settled. But in spite of all that, for many people there was a romance attached to steam trains that diesels never equalled. And for enthusiasts, it was always an exciting moment watching the train approaching the station and waiting to see which engine was pulling it. In fact this particular Castle class 4-6-0 engine, seen here in 1958 and claiming to be the Bristol Castle, had changed identity earlier in the decade. This came about when the official Royal engine, No 4082 Windsor Castle, was awaiting overhaul and so could not be used for the funeral of King George VI in 1952. No 7013 Bristol Castle was substituted, taking on the name and number of the Windsor Castle, and as it turned out this exchange of identities was permanent; the real No 7013 continued to masquerade as No 4082 until 1965, when both engines came to the end of their respective lines.

Above right: The Great Western Railway arrived in West Bromwich in 1854, and until the family car became a fact of life, the railway was an important part of people's daily existence. Today many West Bromwich motorists never catch a train from one year to the next; some of them have only the haziest notion of the places

served, and no idea whatsoever of the timetabling. In the 1950s people who regularly travelled long distances would know the railway timetable practically off by heart; while for others, catching a train meant going on holiday. This particular train is a Saturday South Coast holiday express bringing sun-tanned holidaymakers back to Wolverhampton, and is seen here between West Bromwich and Swan Village. The engine is a Hall class 4-6-0 No 5971 Merevale Hall, one of 330 'Hall' class engines built at Swindon - which, compared to only 171 'Castle' class engines, was quite a lot. Production commenced in 1928, and between 1944 and 1950 modifications carried out to improve their performance resulted in 77 engines which were known - logically enough - as 'Modified Halls'. Examples of both 'Halls' and 'Modified Halls' have been preserved.

Started in 1923, Dartmouth Garages went on to enjoy great success - assisted, no doubt, by polite, soft-sell advertising such as its early-30s proposition: 'May we send a Singer to your home? You incur no obligation'. By 1959 Dartmouth Garage had decided it was time for a facelift, and its new showrooms, where it invited the public to come and see 'beautiful cars in beautiful surroundings', were opened in May 1959. Dartmouth Garage was an Austin dealer, and the beautiful cars seen here include the loveable little 'frog-eyed' Sprite and the luxurious Austin Cambridge. Austin launched seven new models for the 1959 Motor Show, which included the A55 Cambridge Mk II, the Austin Seven, the Austin Healey 3-litre, and a new version of the popular Sprite. Competition among car manufacturers was keen, though; there was the new Triumph Herald, the first car in this country with full independent suspension, or the Ford Anglia, competitively priced at £610. And Russian cars made their first appearance at the '59 Motor Show, with the two-and-a-half-litre Volga and the one-and-a-half-litre Moskvitch epitomising Soviet style.

> *Russian cars made their first appearance at the Motor Show in 1959 with the Volga and the Moskvitch*

A Driving Force in West Bromwich - I.M. Group Limited

I.M. Group Limited owes its existence to a team of people who were formerly Jensen Motors' Limited employees. This team is head up by Robert Edmiston, or Bob as he is known. Born in India in 1946, the son of a British wartime pilot, Bob embarked upon what was to become a hugely successful career in business when at just seventeen years old he took a job as a Bank Clerk. After his brief spell as a Bank Clerk Bob joined Chrysler International as a Treasury Clerk and a year later became a Financial Analyst with the Ford Motor Company. After a sound grounding with Ford, Bob moved onwards again in 1970 joining Chrysler UK where he held a variety of managerial and financial analyst posts. These years of valuable experience won him the post of Financial Controller and Company Secretary for Jensen Motors Limited.

In 1976, when Bob was still only 29 years old, he was faced with the task of winding up Jensen Motors Limited in his role as Financial Director of the company. The collapse of this company provided Bob with an exciting opportunity which, being a dynamic entrepreneur, he was eager to seize.

Therefore, in 1976, Bob combined his redundancy cheque with financial support from his business partner and established Jensen Parts & Service Limited.

Robert Edmiston's new company was immediately successful and in its first year secured a turnover of

Left: Robert Edmiston, founder of the company.
Below: The company's showroom in Ryder Street, West Bromwich in 1980. Bottom: Jensen's Service Shop in Kelvin Way, West Bromwich.

£1million. Indeed, in the May of the same year Bob's impatience to see his company grow initiated his involvement in the former Jensen Parts and Service Limited business. At that time the business which was a fully computerised operation owned an IBM System 3, Model 10 with the core size of 32k. Also in those days, seatbelts were priced as 'extras'!

The first aim of the burgeoning business was to win a car franchise. The aim was achieved in 1977 when the major Japanese company, Fuji Heavy Industries, granted Bob with the Subaru UK car franchise. This was a considerable breakthrough for the company and its introduction of Subaru saloon and estate cars to the UK market was a successful one. Indeed, the company pioneered and helped to create a healthy mass market demand for four-wheel drive passenger cars in the country.

Only three years later in 1980, International Motors Limited was formed, winning the rights to sell Maserati and de Tomaso cars in the UK. This decision was later acknowledged as an error but however, did not repress the continuing achievements of the business but was rather, a

mark of a company willing to take risks in order to succeed. Indeed, in this same year only four years after its establishment, the business had grown so much that it had become too large for its existing premises in West Bromwich. As a consequence the business moved to a new eleven acre site containing offices and old warehouses in Ryder Street. At this time industrial property prices were depressed and this enabled the new premises to be purchased for a shrewd £1.2 million! A further £5 million was later invested in the site which now comprises, up-to-date offices, warehouses and an industrial estate which accommodates over 40 other private businesses.

Merely four years after achieving its initial aim of obtaining a car franchise, in 1981, the company excelled itself by winning the Hyundai franchise. This was achieved in the face of stiff competition from several other major UK

Above left: *Jaguar XK 120 rebuild undertaken by Jensen Motors.* ***Top:*** *Jensen FF undergoing restoration at Service Body Shop.* ***Below:*** *Jensen Intercepter powerplant - Chrysler 7.2 litre V8.*

companies who were just as eager to win the franchise for the UK. The procurement of this franchise made Bob's company the first to import Korean vehicles into the UK market. In doing so, the company turned Hyundai into a household name in Britain. In 1993 Bob decided to sell a controlling interest in the Hyundai franchise to Lex Service plc, initially retaining a 49.9 per cent interest. This was sold to Lex by agreement in 1997.

Keen to sustain the financial security of the company Bob made the astute decision to employ the company's bank manager. This bank manager, from the Bank of America, was assigned the role of Corporate Financial Director and, also at that time, as managing Director of Hyundai.

In 1983 International Motors made the decision to expand its remit, literally even further, into the overseas markets. Subsequently, the company established an overseas subsidiary which was named, VII Limited. The new subsidiary was formed in order to import Subarus into the Republic of Ireland. This aim was accomplished in 1984 and only five years later VII Limited enjoyed the highest market share for Subaru in Europe.

International Motors Limited continued to flourish and in 1984 the company was rewarded for its hard work and success when it received two separate awards. After exhibiting at the British International Motor Show the company was honoured with the 'Most Attractive Stand of the Show' Award. Later, the business received the distinction of being recognised as the 'Top Hyundai Distributor in the World'!

1986 proved to be a landmark year in the history of the company. This was the year of the company's existence. This important 10th anniversary was accordingly marked with a celebratory 'bash' at the Grosvenor House Hotel in

London It was also in this 10th anniversary year that, using the hard-won experience of importing vehicles and a proven ability to launch new franchises, the company scored its car franchise 'hat trick'. It acquired the Isuzu franchise just before Christmas in 1986 from arguably the largest commercial vehicle manufacturer in the world, Isuzu Motors Limited, also Japan's longest established motor manufacturer. This acquisition helped to reinforce International Motors' reputation as a four-wheel drive specialist. Capitalising on its experience and understanding of the needs of the off-road user the company rapidly established Isuzu as a powerful and prestigious name in the four by four market. A year later, in 1987, International Motors launched the Isuzu Trooper. With the help of the company's 100-plus expert dealers the vehicle has been a consistent top-selling recreational vehicle ever since and has become known as a 'workhorse' which also appeals to the aspirational market for fashionable, luxury, lifestyle vehicles.

Below: The company's offices in the 1970s.
Bottom: International Motors' staff in 1976. Robert Edmiston is on the far left.

After the success of purchasing an industrial estate in 1980 another industrial estate was bought, this time in Southampton. It was then that Bob Edmiston set up a property company to run the two estates. I.M. Properties was formed in 1987 as part of the I.M. Group. However, both companies operated separately within the group with their own specialist staff, administrative operations, systems support and financial planning. This arrangement enabled I.M. Properties to benefit from the financial support of the I.M. Group whilst having the freedom to act independently and proved to be a formula for success. The head offices of the property company are situated at the grand and impressive location of Hasely Manor. The 19th century residence dates back to 1066 and once belonged to

Henry VIII. After being renovated, the Manor, strategically located at the heart of the national motorway network just outside Warwick, could be used as the head office for I.M. Properties. It also served as a prestigious income-earning business and conference centre. Indeed, the Manor and Saxon House now contain 48 fully managed office suites accommodating approximately 25 companies in high quality furnished or unfurnished offices with a restaurant, private catering facilities, meeting and board rooms and a range of administrative support systems.

The new property company began by entering the housing market and concentrated on building high specification properties from one bedroom flats to executive homes in desirable, carefully selected locations. The residential side of the company then went on to become one of the first residential developers to sponsor two Business Expansion Schemes (BES). These schemes developed properties to provide cost effective homes for rent which tenants then have the option of purchasing after four years. The company then went on to build a first rate portfolio of prime industrial, retail and residential property.

Business continued to thrive for the I.M. Group. By 1989, VII Limited enjoyed the highest market share for Subaru in

Above left: *Japanese visitors to the premises in 1980.*
Top: *The premises (outlined in white) in the mid-1970s.*

Europe and a year later the Subaru Legacy was voted 'Best Estate Car' by What Car? 'Car of the Year Awards. The company received yet more accolades when in 1992 the Subaru Legacy Turbo was voted 'Best Sporting Saloon' in the What Car? 'Car of the Year Awards', followed by the I.M. stand being awarded the 'Best Stand in Hall 4' at the British International Motor Show. Finally, Subaru's Rally team became British Rally Champions in 1991, 92 and 93!

Whilst these accolades were being won and collected, I.M. Properties was also busy securing success. The investment side of the property business continued acquiring property for both current income and long term potential. In May 1991, the company acquired 28.76 percent of the property company BHH Group Plc and in 1993 took over the balance of shareholding by way of public offer. This was yet another ground-breaking move for the business and in the process increased I.M. Properties' assets from £12 million to in excess of £100 million! The company also acquired fully let industrial/ distribution units located in the M25, M4, M3, 'Golden Triangle'. Also included in the portfolio of the property company are strategically located investments such as the industrial estates at Wakefield, Avonmouth and Bishops Stortford. Another successful industrial estate acquired by the company, which added to its geographically widespread investments, was the Budbrooke Industrial Estate in Warwick. This estate was chosen for the flexibility of its 14 units which varied in size from 1400 to 10000 square feet. During this time I.M. Properties also continued to add substantially to its retail investments acquiring the Longton Exchange Shopping Centre in the Potteries. With its 80 retail units and a high percentage of national multiple retailers in its tenant profile, the centre became I.M.'s largest single retail holding at the time and later underwent a £7 million redevelopment.

In 1993 Bob Edmiston made the decision to sell a controlling interest in International Motors Limited's Hyundai franchise, but retain a 49.9 percent interest. The company that purchased this controlling interest was Lex Service Plc and later, in 1997, they purchased the whole of the Hyundai franchise. This initial decision contributed to the I.M. Group producing an extremely lucrative turnover in 1993 of £227 million!

The I.M. Group launched into 1994 with yet another award. This time, the Subaru Impreza 555 won an Autosport Award for 'Rally Car of the Year'. This success was followed when the company signed an agreement to introduce SsangYong into Britain. SsangYong was a company which had been making four wheel drive trucks and military vehicles for the Asian market since 1954. The SsangYong Musso, designed by the renowned British car designer, Professor Ken Greenley, fitted the International Motors range perfectly. It required the same expertise to sell as the

Above: International Motors' West Bromwich-based staff in the 1980s. Below: The company's first Japanese deal in the 1970s.

Isuzu Trooper whilst filling a complimentary rather than competitive slot in the market. International Motors successfully launched the Musso at the 1994 Motor Show. Also at the show, the SsangYong Musso was awarded the IBCAM British Steel Auto Design Award Gold Medal, completing its successful debut. In 1995, when the Musso went on sale, it exceeded first year sales targets comfortably, with the top specification model, the GSE, selling at twice the anticipated rate.

1994 also proved to be a productive year for I.M. Properties. What was to become the first phase of the 62000 square feet development - Anchor Brook Industrial Park in the West Midlands - was completed. The company conducted a survey of tenant requirements before settling on detailed development specifications. This resulted in all the units being fitted with security and fire alarm systems and CCTV cameras. The other innovative feature of the development was that the 28 acres of mature shrubland and grassland, which formed part of the canalside site, was retained in its natural state in order to protect the area's wild orchids and preserve a habitat for newts and kestrels. Another three units were added to the development in 1998.

Following the success of the Musso, International Motors unveiled a second SsangYong vehicle, named the

Korando, in the following year at the 1995 London Motor Show. In the same year the company was awarded the J D Power and Assocaiates UK Customer Satisfaction Award for the Isuzu Trooper in the 'Sport Utility Vehicle' category. 1995 was also a year of overwhelming success for the 555 Subaru World Rally Team when the team achieved a triple win in the 1995 World Rally Championships in the Impreza Turbo. The team completed this success by taking first, second and third place in the RAC Rally, clinching the Manufacturers' Championship for Subaru and making Colin McRaeWorld Rally Champion and the youngest holder of the title in the sport's history.

Alongside these distinctions, the company progressed further with its continued growth and development. In January 1995 the company expanded its overseas market into Finland. Previously, the I.M. Group had moved into Sweden setting up, International Motors (Sverige) AB, which with its 45 Subaru dealerships is wholly owned by the Group. International Motors (Sverige) AB became

Above: *Betty Boothroyd MP visiting the service department with Mr Edmiston and Terry Hill in 1980.*
Below: *Robert Edmiston outside the company's West Bromwich headquarters with two cars from his Subaru and Hyundai range in 1986.*

the sole distributor for Subaru, Daihatsu and SsangYong and also imports Isuzu spare parts. Finland was chosen because of its position as a strategic gateway to the Baltic countries of Estonia, Latvia and Lithuania. With five months of heavy snow in the south of the country, the climate in Finland was also an advantage for the sales of all-wheel drive vehicles. The move into Finland was marked by the establishment of another overseas subsidiary, International Motors Suomi Oy. Like the other subsidiaries Suomi Oy was set up to operate separately with its own training and marketing resources. The Properties side of the company was not to be left behind in this year and it purchased the 160000 square feet Richmond Centre Shopping Complex in Londonderry for £15.75million, overtaking the Longton Exchange as I.M.'s largest single retail holding.

By the time the I.M. Group celebrated its 20th anniversary in 1996, the company had come a long way. From the £1 million turnover in the first year of trading, the company was now reaching a turnover of £193.5 million with the value of capitals and reserves totalling £135 million. This anniversary year was also an impressive one for awards. The company won the JD Power and Associates UK Customer Satisfaction Award for the Isuzu Trooper in the 'Sport Utility Vehicle Category'; the IBCAM British Steel Auto Design Award Gold Medal for the SsangYong Musso; and Subaru also retained the World Rally Championship Manufacturers' title. The company also won the 'Secured By Design' award for I.M. Properties Junction Six Industrial Park development. This development comprised, a 32 acre

industrial estate in Birmingham adjacent to Junction six of the M6 with 500000 square feet of industrial , distribution and business space. The investment side of the Properties business also increased its holding in the South East at this time with the purchase of a £17.6 million investment from Hermes, the Post Office/British Telecom pension fund. In the meantime, the residential side of the business gave a substantial grant to the Warwickshire Museum to fund an archaeological excavation and survey.

International Motors' success in the J.D. Power and Associates UK Customer Satisfaction Study reached new

Above: *The NEC Motor Show in 1992 with the Duke of Kent at the Hyundai stand.* ***Top:*** *I.M. Properties' Junction Six development in Birmingham.*

heights in 1997 when Subaru won the 1st place Gold Award for the top manufacturer.

In 1998 the Korean company Daewoo took over the running of SsangYong and as a result the I.M. Group stopped marketing these models. However, later the same year, in the Spring of 1998, the company launched the Korean Daewoo brand into Sweden. During this year the total value of sales and purchases for I.M. Properties was close to £90 million, encouraged by the acquisitions of Yorkshire Holdings Limited, Shop Investments Nationwide Limited and Shop Investments Property Trading Limited. This increasing success gave the company the freedom to operate independently when, in this year, the de-merger of I.M. Properties from the I.M. Group took place. A year later, in 1999, I.M. Properties started work on its largest development to date. The development of the 339 acre site at Birch Coppice, Tamworth makes it the second largest development of its kind in the Midlands. With its ideal location, near to

Junction 10 of the M42, the site provides 2000000 square feet of industrial, office and manufacturing space.

Also in 1999, Subaru again won the top manufacturers 1st place Gold Award in the J.D. Power and Associates UK Customer Satisfaction Awards. Furthermore, the Subaru Impreza and Legacy were 1st and 2nd in the model by model survey.

After increasing in strength during one of the toughest periods in the car industry the I.M. Group plans to continue to grow and succeed in the future. The company's high standards will help towards this aim. The assurance of product quality; the commitment to building long term business relationships; the readily accessible executives to staff, customers and business partners; the solid core of skills and experience; the respected financial track record; the successful marketing and PR skills; and the re-investment of profits are amongst the long list of things that will ensure that I.M. Group Limited continues to be a driving force in the future. Bob Edmiston's company has become one of the fastest growing private companies in the country. The second generation of Edmiston's, Bob's son Andrew, has now joined his father in the business as the Managing Director of I.M. Truck (UK) Limited. Indeed, despite Bob's many interests including: running the charitable trust 'Christian Vision'; windsurfing; skiing; flying; and shooting, Bob's entrepreneurial spirit will no doubt carry his company forward to face many more challenges and successes in the future.

Above: *Subaru (UK) Limited supported Esther Rantzen in her Childline Appeal.* ***Below:*** *Jilly Goolden seen here with Mr Edmiston and Mr SJ Kim (Chief Executive and Chairman of SsangYong Motor Company) at the 1994 Birmingham Motor Show.*

Below: The Wesleyan Chapel was demolished in September 1972, the nearby Tower is gone too, and the road layout is now somewhat different, but Farley Clock Tower has been a landmark at Carters Green for more than a century. As the inscription around the four sides of the 65 feet high tower tells us, it was erected in recognition of Alderman Ruben Farley, West Bromwich's first mayor. However, although externally the tower and clock face may look just the same as they did in 1897, the innards are different. In 1973 the clock's workings were overhauled and electric winding gear was put in, which means that the weekly exercise of climbing the 43 steps in order to wind the clock is no longer necessary now that the clock is driven by electricity. The clean and overhaul cost £1,040, as compared to the original cost of erecting the clock in 1897 - £800, raised by public subscription.

Right: West Bromwich kept its trams until 1939. By this time it had been operating electric trams for 37 years, and even when these were introduced in 1902 trams themselves were nothing new. The tramway itself had been constructed in the early 1870s and the town had come to rely first on horse-drawn trams and then, from 1883, on steam trams. By 1937 only people with very long memories indeed could remember West Bromwich without trams, so when it was announced in the summer of that year that all the trams on the Birmingham and West Bromwich network were to be replaced by 'oil' omnibuses, it took a while to get used to the idea. There had also been talk of trolley buses - such as operated in Wolverhampton for 44 years - but in the end 'oil' buses won the vote and took over the 7,454 miles of the network. The last Saturday night tram ran through West Bromwich in March 1939, and Sunday morning travellers had their first experience of the new omnibus service. The general verdict was that the 'buses were warmer, but they didn't make the nice soothing clickety-clack rhythm that you got with the trams!

Around the town centre

Events of the 1940s

MELODY MAKERS
The songs of radio personalities such as Bing Crosby and Vera Lynn were whistled, sung and hummed everywhere during the 1940s. The 'forces' sweetheart' brought hope to war-torn Britain with 'When the Lights go on Again', while the popular crooner's 'White Christmas' is still played around Christmas time even today. Who can forget songs like 'People Will Say we're in Love', 'Don't Fence Me In', 'Zip-a-dee-doo-dah', and 'Riders in the Sky'?

INVENTION AND TECHNOLOGY
Inspired by quick-drying printers' ink, in 1945 Hungarian journalist Laszlo Biro developed a ballpoint pen which released viscous ink from its own reservoir as the writer moved the pen across the page. An American inventor was working on a similar idea at the same time, but it was Biro's name that stuck. A few years later Baron Bich developed a low cost version of the pen, and the 'Bic' ballpoint went on sale in France in 1953.

SCIENCE AND DISCOVERY
In 1943 Ukrainian-born biochemist Selman Abraham Waksman made a significant discovery. While studying organisms found in soil he discovered an antibiotic (a name Waksman himself coined) which was later found to be the very first effective treatment for tuberculosis. A major killer for thousands of years, even the writings of the ancient Egyptians contain stories of people suffering from tuberculosis. Waksman's development of streptomycin brought him the 1952 Nobel Prize for Medicine.

H Geddes clearly placed great faith in bus advertising, with two out of two buses on this shot from around 1960 spreading the word on their behalf. Around this time, however, more and more travellers were beginning to rely on private cars, rather than buses; by 1963 a national average one person out of seven would own a car. This nationwide switch from public transport to private has also led to the growth of out-of-town trading, and a

number of major chain stores - including Marks & Spencer, just visible here beyond Burtons - subsequently opted to move out to large purpose-built premises on retail parks: handy for the motorist, but less so for the bus passenger. The name Marks & Spencer first appeared above a store up in Darlington in 1922, although in fact the business began as far back as 1894. Founders Michael Marks and Tom Spencer opened their first shops under the name of Penny Bazaar, and by 1915 Messrs Marks and Spencer had set up 140 Penny Bazaars throughout the country - not a bad rate of return from an investment of £300, representing a half-share in the enterprise!

This shot was taken looking down High Street from the direction of Carters Green, with the distinctive spire of St Michael's indicating where St Michael's Street meets High Street. Now that we can no longer drive along High Street from end to end we tend to forget just how long it actually is; it covers a distance of one and a quarter miles, from Carters Green to Birmingham Road. It was the Golden Mile, the stretch where the most popular shops were to be found, which attracted the attention of the town planners in the 1960s. The section north of St Michael's Street which we see here has remained relatively unaltered, architecturally speaking. The road still carries traffic in both directions, going to and from the ring road, and the line of gabled buildings pictured here is still there, although its occupants have changed in line with the overall philosophy of concentrating retailers within the designated shopping precinct. So The Louvre - the household department store which used to stock an excellent range of Ladybird clothes for our little ones - has been split up into smaller units again, and at the time of writing the businesses located in this block include banks, a bookies and a nightclub.

> **Between 1953 and 1963 the number of cars rose from one car for every 24 people to one for every seven**

Above: This view of a traffic line-up in Paradise Street is dated circa 1960, although the prevalence of 1950s models suggests that it could in fact be slightly earlier. Be that as it may, a generation is growing up which takes the motor car for granted; between 1953 and 1963 the number of private cars in the country rose from one car for every twenty-four people to one for every seven. Driving schools flourished during the 60s - although the L-plate tied to the bumper of the Morris Eight suggests that in this case official driving lessons are being dispensed with; let us hope that no major domestic rows blew up as a result! For the younger generation, passing your test became a rite of passage. In fact the driving test, along with L-plates and provisional licences, was first introduced in 1935, initially on a voluntary basis; it then became compulsory, and everybody who had taken out their first driving licence since 1st April 1934 was obliged to take a test. The test fee was initially set at 7/6 (37.5p), but the Driving Test Organisation was so honest that when it discovered it had unintentionally made a profit of £16,000, it reduced the fee.

Below: A prodigal son returning to West Bromwich after half a century's absence might not recognise a great deal in the view looking down High Street from Dartmouth Square today, but at least he would find the clock where he left it (though if clocks could talk, it would have its own tale to tell). There can be few shopping centres in Britain situated closer to a motorway than the centre of West Bromwich is to the M5, and it is not difficult to imagine the kind of scenarios that could have arisen if the ever-increasing volume of motorway traffic had been allowed to continue using the full length of High Street as its through route. As it is, the problem has been averted and the town's proximity to the motorway has been turned into an advantage instead of a nightmare - you can be happily doing your shopping in the Farley Centre within minutes of exiting from the M5.

Bottom: In 1965, when this photograph was taken, the pavement on the side of Bull Street with the shops on could expect an average of 1,110 pedestrians an hour to walk along it (according to a survey of pedestrian movements in May 1964). However, Bull Street fell outside the main retail shopping zone in West Bromwich's redevelopment plans; the east side was earmarked as offices, and today, with lanes of ringway traffic rushing along in a southerly direction, it seems unlikely that 1,110 pedestrians a week would choose to amble along here, let alone 1,110 pedestrians an hour. This, of course, was the planners' intention; the masterplan was to ensure that shoppers would find everything they needed within the central pedestrianised shopping area. The Council actively encouraged a good mix of shops, recognising that some types of outlet had been overrepresented at the expense of others in the old Golden Mile and seeking to redress the balance. Those of us who have grown up with the slick gyratory system and the modern shopping precincts take the present layout very much for granted and find it hard to imagine our town any other way, but we should not forget how much planning and hard work went into its creation.

These two shots of High Street were both taken looking north-west from Dartmouth Square in 1965, and show the shops which used to stand along either side of the street. The buildings in the foreground of the 'left-hand' side (how many readers bought their wedding cake from Broadheads on this spot?) have all disappeared, to be replaced by the Farley Centre. However, once we pass the Sandwell Centre and get down into Duchess Parade, the Great Western and a number of its near neighbours are still with us, rubbing shoulders with the new MacDonalds, while at the far end the Star and Garter has been promoted to a prime corner position through the demolition of the rest of the row which used to stand between it and St Michael's Street. On the 'right-hand' side, the story is a little more complicated; the Queens Square development is set back from a building line now composed of a mixture of original and redeveloped buildings. Prior to the regeneration scheme, the majority of the buildings which stood along the length of High Street had been erected earlier than 1857. Today, West Bromwich is an intriguing blend of old and new - ornate 19th-century gabled buildings facing modern office blocks, old premises converted to new uses, traditional industries finding new applications - and this ability to adapt without losing touch with the past is an important part of the town's character.

Plenty of old familiar names adorn the shopfronts in this 1965 view of High Street, including Dorothy Perkins, Halfords, the Co-op and the Singer shop. Singer sewing machines used to be an essential piece of equipment to most women and girls during the 1950s and 60s, and the Singer shop, with its dress patterns, fabrics, buttons and other accessories, was an important port of call for every nimble-fingered enthusiast. This was the heyday of home sewing. Simplicity, Style and Maudella were the favourite paper patterns to buy, and many were the dresses, skirts and blouses created on the kitchen table during those busy evenings and weekends. Children went to school proudly dressed in Mum's creations, home-sewn curtains hung at our

Events of the 1950s

WHAT'S ON?
Television hit Britain in a big way during the 1950s. Older readers will surely remember 'Double Your Money, Dixon of Dock Green and 'Dragnet' (whose characters' names were changed 'to protect the innocent'). Commercial television was introduced on 22nd September 1955, and Gibbs SR toothpaste were drawn out of the hat to become the first advert to be shown. Many believed adverts to be vulgar, however, and audiences were far less than had been hoped for.

GETTING AROUND
The year 1959 saw the development of the world's first practical air-cushion vehicle - better known to us as the hovercraft. The earliest model was only able to travel at slow speeds over very calm water and was unable to carry more than three passengers. The faster and smoother alternative to the sea ferry quickly caught on, and by the 1970s a 170-ton car-carrying hovercraft service had been introduced across the English Channel.

SPORTING CHANCE
The four-minute mile had remained the record since 1945, and had become regarded as virtually unbreakable. On 6th May 1954, however, Oxford University student Roger Bannister literally ran away with the record, accomplishing the seemingly impossible in three minutes 59.4 seconds. Bannister collapsed at the end of his last amazing lap, even temporarily losing his vision. By the end of the day, however, he had recovered sufficiently to celebrate his achievement in a London night club!

windows, and our living room sofas and armchairs were liberally strewn with brightly coloured cushions. Then the time came when it was as cheap to buy clothes as to make them; so we did, and many a sewing machine was consigned to the attic where its once-cherished wooden cases gradually mildewed and the metal parts, which we used to anoint lovingly with special sewing-machine oil to ensure smooth running, developed spots of rust.

Events of the 1950s

HOT OFF THE PRESS

The 1950s seemed to be the heyday of spies, and in 1951 the activities of Guy Burgess and Donald Maclean caused a sensation in the country. Both had occupied prominent positions in the Foreign Office, while Burgess had also been a member of MI-6. Recruited by the Russians while at Cambridge University in the 1930s, the traitors provided the Soviets with a huge amount of valuable information. They disappeared in 1951, surfacing in Moscow five years later.

THE WORLD AT LARGE

Plans to develop the economies of member states into one common market came to fruition on 1st January 1958, when the EEC came into operation. The original members were France, Belgium, Luxembourg, The Netherlands, Italy, and West Germany. The Community became highly successful, achieving increased trade and prosperity across Western Europe while at the same time alleviating fear of war which lingered on after the end of World War II. Britain became a member in 1973.

SCIENCE AND DISCOVERY

DNA (deoxyribonucleic acid) was first defined as long ago as 1953, and the effects have been far-reaching. The key discovery was developed over the following years and today DNA fingerprinting has become an accepted part of life. Genetic diseases such as hemophilia and cystic fibrosis have been identified. Criminals are continually detected and brought to justice. Biological drugs have been developed. More controversially, drought and disease-resistant plants have been engineered - and Dolly the sheep has been produced.

Make light meals lighter - drinka pinta, urges the Midland Counties milk float parked outside the market arcade. The Drinka Pinta Milka Day campaign was launched in 1958, reputedly in the face of strong opposition from some of the advertising executives involved who thought it was an absolutely dreadful slogan. Although some teachers and parents expressed horror and disgust at seeing the English language mangled in this way, it became one of the classic pieces of advertising, and the word 'pinta' now appears in practically every

English dictionary. A whole series of 'pinta' slogans followed, though on reflection this particular one seems a little obscure - how exactly does drinking a pinta make a meal lighter? Especially when skimmed and semi-skimmed milk was the exception rather than the rule . . . Beyond the milk float we have Woolworths, the American company which translated its original '5 and 10 cent Stores' tag into '3d and 6d Stores' when it estab-lished itself in the UK. The original '5 and 10 cent Stores' had spread across America towards the end of the 19th century ever since F W Woolworth had opened his first stores selling a wide range of goods at fixed low prices in 1879. By 1911 he had a chain of over 1,000 shops in the USA, and he and his brother C S Woolworth subsequently expanded into the UK, Canada and Europe.

Above: On this distinctly damp and miserable-looking day in 1960, Paradise Street has little chance of living up to its name. The old-style bus shelters which lined the street gave limited protection from the elements - none at all, if the wind was blowing from the wrong direction - and of a cold rainy evening, after a visit to the cinema, The Grapes might well have seemed a more attractive place to wait for your bus. A few doors along from The Grapes is an advert which proclaims: Your paper is The Despatch. The Evening Despatch first appeared in 1891. Having kept the good people of West Bromwich informed about the state of the nation through trade depressions, Royal events, political controversy and two world wars, as well as guiding them through the intricacies of countless local crises, triumphs and debates, The Despatch, along with the other local newspapers - of which the only Midlands-based morning paper was The Birmingham Post - had already made reference to the radical changes which were in store for the centre of West Bromwich over the coming decade - and which would transform this particular street beyond recognition.

Left: Local brewers Mitchell & Butler, based in Cape Hill, certainly had Dartmouth Square all sewn up, with the Bull's Head (on the left-hand side of the photograph) and, opposite, the Dartmouth Hotel both bearing its distinctive M&B logo. The Ford waiting at the lights is, we think, a Prefect, although at this distance in time appearances could deceive. Originally the Prefect and the Anglia shared this body shape, with the Prefect being distinguishable by its additional chrome trim. However, in 1960 - four years before this photograph was taken - the more angular 'New Anglia' was introduced, and the old Anglia turned into the 'New Popular'. At the same time the 'New Prefect' was introduced, which looked the same as the old Prefect, but had a new engine. No doubt this sounds confusing to younger readers, though to those of us who were there at the time it seemed to make perfect sense! Also well worth a mention in this picture is The China Shop, just this side of Keys, with its entire front wall covered with the names of the prestigious ranges of pottery products which it sold.

The spire of St Michael's Church is no longer visible from this spot; the view is blocked by shop canopies, while what was formerly the middle of High Street - the horse road, as we used to call it - is now populated by a colourful array of stalls down the centre of the precinct. W H Smith now occupies the spot where the Co-op used to be. During the second half of the 19th century West Bromwich had a number of small local Co-operative Societies, but it was not until the early 20th century that the Co-op estab-

lished a presence in High Street. After a series of amalgamations, the West Bromwich branches of the Co-operative became part of the Birmingham Society in 1925, although the Walsall and District Co-operative Society also moved into the town during the 30s. The Birmingham Society made plans to build a new departmental store in West Bromwich High Street in the 1930s, but this project, like so many others, was interrupted by the war and the premises were not completed until the mid-50s.

Events of the 1950s

MELODY MAKERS
Few teenage girls could resist the blatant sex-appeal of 'Elvis the Pelvis', though their parents were scandalised at the moody Presley's provocatively gyrating hips. The singer took America and Britain by storm with such hits as 'Jailhouse Rock', 'All Shook Up' and 'Blue Suede Shoes'. The rhythms of Bill Haley and his Comets, Buddy Holly and Chuck Berry turned the 1950s into the Rock 'n' Roll years.

INVENTION AND TECHNOLOGY
Until the late 1950s you did not carry radios around with you. Radios were listened to at home, plugged into a mains socket in every average sitting room. Japan was in the forefront of electronic develop-ments even then, and in 1957 the Japanese company Sony introduced the world's very first all-transistor radio - an item of new technology that was small enough to fit into your pocket. The major consumer product caught on fast - particularly with teenage listeners.

ROYAL WATCH
King George VI's health had been causing problems since 1948, when he developed thrombosis. In 1951 the King - always a heavy smoker - became ill again, and was eventually found to be suffering from lung cancer. His left lung was removed in September of 1951. In January 1952 he waved Princess Elizabeth and Prince Philip off on their tour of Africa; they were never to see him again. The King died in the early hours of 6th February 1952.

This junction is completely different today; the only recognisable feature which has survived from 1960 is St Michael's Church, to the right. The building line on the south side of St Michael's Street has been taken right back to make way for the dual carriageway, and there is now a pedestrian subway on the corner once occupied by Barklays and their nine furniture showrooms, which they so proudly invited you to walk around. Beyond Barklays the old railway booking office is visible, and beyond

that, the Army Information Office. At around the time this picture was taken, the Army, along with the other armed services, was having to work on its image to promote itself as a good career for a young man. The end of National Service made the Forces reliant on voluntary recruitment from late 1960 on; the last batch of enlistment notices went out in November 1960. Those not cut out for military life who had escaped being called up breathed a sigh of relief, but for others, the opportunity to see the world was sufficiently attractive for them to join up anyway. And then there was the hard core who insisted that National Service should never have been stopped - Army discipline was the only way to stop us turning into a nation of hooligans and juvenile delinquents . . .

Anyone who had just torn themself away from a smart suit in Burtons or Marks & Spencer that they desperately wanted but couldn't afford might have gazed longingly at the slogan on the bus: Two more £75,000 winners in one week on Littlewoods. Although it very rarely is you, the important thing is that it might be, next time. This photograph was taken in August 1957, so Littlewoods and their old rivals Vernons now had new competition: on 1st June the Electronic Random Number Indicator had chosen the winning numbers in the first £5,000 prize draw.

How many readers still have an Ernie, we wonder - and how many of those actually know their Premium Bond number? Now, of course, we have the National Lottery in all its various forms - twice-weekly draws, lucky dips, scratch cards, you pays your money and takes your choice - but many people still enjoy the weekly ritual of filling in the pools coupon. The successful Littlewoods mail order and football pools business started in Liverpool and went on to make a fortune for its founder, Manchester-born Sir John Moore, who began his working life as a messenger boy.

On the home front

> *In all, some 40 acres of land were acquired by the Council to build the Ringway*

Queen Street was chopped in two by the Ringway, and the part inside the magic ring was redeveloped as Queen's Square. In all, some 40 acres of buildings and land were acquired by compulsory purchase orders to allow the plans to proceed, and the Council estimated that the total cost of acquisition and development would be over £7 million; those of an arithmetical turn of mind may care to know that the redevelopment area covered more than 77 acres, and comprised 385 shops, 470 dwellings, 21 pubs, 7 churches, 3 cinemas, 1 fire station and 1 market hall. The importance of keeping a healthy mixture of residential and retail use was recognised, and so the original plans made provision for 600 flats and maisonettes to accommodate families with no children; this was felt to be essential in order to prevent the town becoming unhealthily depopulated when the day's trading ended. It was at a much later stage of the work, in 1974, that the novel idea of putting pensioners in penthouses on top of the Dartmouth Square development was proposed.

The housing programme was in full swing again. Between 1939 and 1945 building had stopped, and by the end of the war there were 5,662 applicants on the waiting list for housing. Then post-war production was stepped up to a rate of more than 150 dwellings a years, and all over West Bromwich families were eagerly awaiting the good news that they had been allocated a house. But when Mr and Mrs James Whitehouse's turn came, there was a little extra surprise in store for them; they had been allocated number 20, Sutton Crescent. and it just so happened that this was the 1,000th Corporation House to be completed by West Bromwich's

Public Works Department. Accordingly, on the afternoon of 14th September 1960 an official ceremony was held, and the couple were met on the doorstep by the Mayor, Councillor Mrs Doris Manifold, and Alderman J D Davis, Chairman of the Public Works Committee. Alderman Davis handed over number 20, Sutton Crescent to the Mayor, and the house was then declared available for inspection. The ceremony concluded at four o'clock, and tea was then served in the Town Hall; after which we presume that Mr and Mrs Whitehouse were finally able to begin settling into their new home.

Below: The construction of Hall Green estate was a major achievement. West Bromwich desperately needed new housing, and for those who had had to live in overcrowded, substandard accommodation, perhaps sharing with in-laws who themselves were on the waiting list for a Corporation house, the prospect of living in a veritable mansion such as this must have seemed like a dream. Of course, not all the properties on Hall Green looked like the one pictured here. This particular des res, with its gables, bay windows and fancy brickwork, could well be one of those built on Westminster Road, and all around it houses were being constructed in a variety of styles and sizes. There were flat-fronted houses, houses with porches, houses with ground-floor bays and houses with two-storey bays; there were semis, short terraces, longer terraces, maisonettes and flats; in fact, there were properties designed to accommodate every type of tenant from the young couple with a large and growing family to the elderly. In all, the Corporation created 25 post-war housing estates and accommodated people in five and a half thousand new houses as well as 210 other properties and 15 converted flats which it had acquired. Things were definitely looking up in West Bromwich as far as housing was concerned - though for those near the bottom of the list, seeing other people moving into houses like this must have made the waiting seem even worse.

Bottom: Readers who are familiar with Carrington Road as it looks today will immediately spot that it has changed a little since 1950. The trees have grown bigger, for one thing; for another, traffic calming measures have turned the road into a chicane of width restrictors and bollards, while the approach roads are guarded by vicious concrete humps. It was inevitable that a wide, straight road such as this would turn into a race-track, and it is easy to say, with hindsight, that the planners should have foreseen the problems of speeding vehicles along a street built to accommodate families with young children; but when Carrington Road was designed there just weren't as many cars on the road, boy-racers were a new phenomenon, joy-riding barely existed and the offence of 'twoc', or 'taking without consent', had not been coined. And certainly the wide expanse of road and pavement conjured up a great sense of luxury and affluence - Carrington Boulevard would have been a more suitable name!

Events of the 1960s

WHAT'S ON?

Television comedy came into its own in the 1960s, and many of the shows that were favourites then went on to become classics. 'On the Buses', 'Steptoe and Son', 'Till Death Us Do Part' and 'The Army Game' kept audiences laughing, while the incredible talents of Morecambe and Wise, the wit of Des O'Connor - often the butt of the duo's jokes - and the antics of Benny Hill established them for ever in the nation's affections.

GETTING AROUND

The 2nd March 1969 was a landmark in the history of aviation. The Anglo-French supersonic airliner Concorde took off for the first time from Toulouse in France. Concorde, which can cruise at almost twice the speed of sound, was designed to fly from London to New York in an incredible three hours twenty minutes. The event took place just weeks after the Boeing 747, which can carry 500 passengers to Concorde's modest 100, made its first flight.

SPORTING CHANCE

Wembley Stadium saw scenes of jubilation when on 30th July 1966 England beat West Germany 4-2 in the World Cup. The match, played in a mixture of sunshine and showers, had been a nailbiting experience for players and spectators alike from the very beginning when Germany scored only thirteen minutes into the game. It was Geoff Hurst's two dramatic goals scored in extra time that secured the victory and lifted the cup for England - at last.

At the microphone is Mr Lewis Silkin, MP, the Minister of Town and Country Planning, and he is giving a speech on the occasion of the opening of the last house on Harvills Hawthorn No 1 Estate on May 31st, 1948. This was the first West Bromwich housing estate to be completed since the war. The 35-acre, formerly derelict site upon which it was built had been acquired by West Bromwich Council and levelled prior to 1939, but work had then been suspended for the duration of the war and the first house was finally ready in July 1946. The 450 houses, of which

more than half were brick built and 150 were permanent British Steel Construction prefabs, were designed to accommodate a mixture of households; for instance, accommodation for couples was built above old people's flats. A great deal of care had gone into the planning, with more attention was being paid to the provision of amenities than had been the case in many pre-war construction projects. In all, some seven acres had been set aside for a primary school, a church, shops and communal buildings. The new awareness of, and interest in, social issues was reflected in Mr Silkin's speech. It was wrong, he observed, 'for women to travel at least two miles to do their shopping . . . Under such conditions it is no wonder that wives do not want their husbands to come home for their midday meals.'

This photograph of Newtown housing estate was taken in August 1950. Housing had been a very emotive issue in West Bromwich for decades - some might say that it still is. A great deal of progress had been made in the five years between 1945 and 1950, with a total of almost 25,300 houses being built in the areas of the 40 local authorities in the West Midlands. This included all sizes and types of houses, of which the great majority were Council houses, while some 4,000 of them were private houses built under licence. Of the Council housing, more than 18,000 were permanent dwellings, and around 3,000 were temporary, prefab style structures. Twenty-five thousand houses sounds a lot, but with the area's population standing at around 1,174,000, this still only equates to one new house between forty-five people. Although the Council had formulated a clear policy on how to allocate properties, feeling ran high on occasion, giving rise to indignant letters to the paper highlighting particular cases and complaining about the disgraceful injustice of letting a three-bedroom house to a couple with one child, while some families still had to sleep five to a bedroom.

Golden Years of **WEST BROMWICH**

Shopping spree

Never mind traffic congestion, pedestrian congestion seems to be the problem on this 1965 shot of High Street, by Scotland Passage. The bus queues are practically blocking the pavement, and shoppers have to battle their way through the crush - no wonder the lady walking towards the camera is clutching her handbag tightly in front of her with a look of grim determination on her face! However, judging by the headscarves, coats and boots, it would seem to be a cold day, so the body heat would not come amiss to those waiting for their bus. Bangers and mash would make a quick, warming meal when they get home, and conveniently situated on the opposite side of High Street is a branch of Palethorpe's, the Dudley-based sausage manufacturer whose special varieties, such as Royal Cambridge sausages, were favourites of the nation. Palethorpe's was founded in 1852 and continued making sausages at Dudley Port until 1966. People might remember some of their advertisements, including the ones which invited you to draw your own conclusions as to the best sausages, and showed pigs pulling along strings of sausages . . . drawing, as it were, their own conclusions!

If some of these gentlemen were being dragged on a shopping expedition by their wives, under protest, to buy themselves a new suit, they could look forward to a long day of it. One thing High Street was not short of was gentlemen's tailors. On the corner was John Collier; further down was Zissman, then Dunn & Co (who began as hatmakers), then Burtons, to name just a few. Many readers will no doubt remember the jolly little TV jingle that informed viewers that John Colliers was 'the window to watch'! Colliers took over the rival firm FST, alias the Fifty Shilling Tailors, a chain which was established during the 1920s and supplied many servicemen

Events of the 1960s

HOT OFF THE PRESS
Barbed wire, concrete blocks and a wide no-man's-land divided East from West when a reinforced wall was built right across the city of Berlin in 1961. Many East Germans escaped to the West at the eleventh hour, taking with them only the possessions they could carry. The Berlin Wall divided the city - and hundreds of family members and friends - for 28 years until the collapse of Communist rule across Eastern Europe. Who can ever forget those scenes in 1989, when ordinary people themselves began to physically tear down the hated wall?

THE WORLD AT LARGE
'One giant leap for mankind' was taken on 20th July 1969, when Neil Armstrong made history as the first man to set foot on the moon. During the mission he and fellow-astronaut 'Buzz' Aldrin collected rock and soil samples, conducted scientific experiments - and had a lot of fun jumping around in the one-sixth gravity. Twenty-one hours and thirty-seven minutes after their landing they took off again in their lunar module 'Eagle' to rejoin Apollo II which was orbiting above them, proudly leaving the American flag on the Moon's surface.

ROYAL WATCH
Princess Margaret's announcement in 1960 that she was to wed photographer Antony Armstrong-Jones (later Lord Snowdon) brought sighs of relief from her immediate family. Just five years earlier the people of Britain had sympathised as the princess bowed to public and private pressure, ending her relationship with Peter Townsend, Prince Philip's former equerry. The Church (and the Queen, as its Head) frowned on the liaison as Townsend was divorced. Her marriage to Lord Snowdon itself ended in 1978.

with affordable suits of a perfectly acceptable quality. Gentlemen's outfitting has long been a trade to attract rivals, from the bottom end of the market upwards: Alkit (who specialised in cheaper clothing), Greenwoods, Hepworths (who eventually managed to acquire the services of the Queen's own designer), Hornes, Moss Bros, Austin Reed, Hector Powe - the list goes on and on.

The decades of the 1950s and 60s were the heyday of television, record players and the transistor radio, and business was booming for shops such as this one. Gone were the days when the 'wireless' was a large piece of equipment that stood on the sideboard in the lounge, and had to be plugged in and allowed to warm up before the plummy tones of the BBC presenter could be heard. The transistor radio meant immediate and portable - if sometimes rather tinny - sound, and the popularity of these novel miniature radios spread like the 'flu. No self-respecting teenager wanted be seen without the 'tranny' that had become the latest fashion accessory. It

was the 'in' gift that Santa left under many a tree - 'Pick a Pye for Christmas' was an oft-seen advert during the run up to the festive season - while for those whom Santa had ignored, the sign advertising FREE trannies was surely too good to ignore! Pocket-sized transistor radios had been developed by the Japanese company Sony as early as 1952, though it took a few more years before companies such as Pye made them widely available in Britain at a price that most people could afford. Another poster in the same window is advertising the Dansette record player, another must-have for trendy guys and chicks.

This photograph, looking south-east along High Street, between Queen Street and Hudson's Passage, provides clear evidence of what the problem was and why something had to be done about it. The pavement simply wasn't wide enough to take this volume of shoppers, and although the likely lads who have been forced to step out into the roadway don't seem particularly bothered by the fact that a double-decker bus is approaching, the situation in 1965 was clearly far from ideal and road accidents were just waiting

High Street was officially the busiest stretch of pavement in the town

to happen. In fact this was officially the busiest stretch of pavement in town. A survey of pedestrian movements in the centre of West Bromwich had been conducted in May of the previous year, with census stations set up at strategic points along the streets, and the highest number of pedestrians had been counted passing along the north side of High Street between Queen Street and Bull Street, with the second highest number on the south side of the same stretch of High Street.

At work

Before the days of mass television advertising, exhibitions provided traders and manufacturers with a useful opportunity to draw public attention to their products. The British Industries Fair at Castle Bromwich was one of the major annual trade events, but a great many smaller exhibitions were put on locally. For instance, the Dudley & District Trades & Industries Exhibition in the National Projectile Factory at Waddams Pool provided a platform for over 80 exhibitors, with a band and a circus to attract visitors. On a smaller scale, in November 1932 Gripton's Radio Store of 309 High Street held a Wireless Exhibition in Ruskin Hall, on the corner of High Street and Lombard Street, where they displayed their range of Ekco consolettes, Marconiphone radiograms and other state-of-the-art offerings.

The precise date and location of the Izons exhibition stand seen here are not known. Izons, the well-known holloware manufacturer, was one of West Bromwich's longest-established companies. Around the turn of the 19th century they were doing such a good trade in rice bowls for India that 200 moulders were kept continuously employed in making them. By 1948 Izons was producing around three-quarters of Britain's total output of cast-iron holloware. It is to this fine West Bromwich company that we owe the first locking handles for pans - more secure than the riveted-on handles - and also the process of casting kettles and spouts all in one operation, to prevent leaky spouts. The star of the stage here is the Eyes On cooker - and what a well-built piece of work it was, too.

Events of the 1960s

MELODY MAKERS
The 1960s: those were the days when the talented blues guitarist Jimi Hendrix shot to rock stardom, a youthful Cliff Richard charmed the nation with his 'Congratulations' and Sandie Shaw won the Eurovision Song Contest for Britain with 'Puppet on a String'. It was the combined musical talents of a group of outrageous working-class Liverpool lads, however, who formed the Beatles and took the world by storm with music that ranged from the experimental to ballads such as 'Yesterday'.

INVENTION AND TECHNOLOGY
A major step forward was made in 1960 when the laser was invented. An acronym for Light Amplification by Stimulated Emission of Radiation, the device produces a narrow beam of light that can travel for vast distances and is focused to give enormous power. Laser beams, as well as being able to carry far more information than radio waves, can also be used for surgery, cutting, drilling, welding and scores of other operations.

SCIENCE AND DISCOVERY
When the drug Thalidomide was first developed during the 1950s it was hailed as a wonder drug which would ease the distressing symptoms of pregnancy sickness. By the early 1960s the drug's terrible side effects were being discovered, when more than 3000 babies had been born with severe birth defects. Malformed limbs, defective eyes and faulty intestines were the heart-rending legacy left by Thalidomide.

In our more enlightened day and age, both sexes can take CDT and Home Economics, but it used to be woodwork and metalwork for the boys and Domestic Science for the girls. These industrious lads are pupils of Churchfields High School, and they are fortunate in that Churchfields had particularly well-equipped laboratories and workshops. Opened in the mid-50s by Sir Hartley Shawcross QC MP, Churchfields was seen as a flagship for the future of education in West Bromwich. It was the town's first big comprehensive school, with a planned 12-form entry of between 1,700 and 1,800 pupils drawn from

the catchment area around Great Barr and Hamstead. To prevent anonymity in such a large establishment, a 'House' system was introduced, with each pupil being allocated to one of ten 'Houses'; this encouraged competition and also separated pupils into smaller units where their welfare and social development could be overseen by the housemaster. In order to attract top quality teaching staff during a national shortage of teachers, the post of Head carried with it an allowance of £730 over and above the basic teaching scales for a man, with an extra £250 for the Deputy Head and £150 for each Head of Department. The buildings and the layout of the school, too, were considered very attractive; in fact, Churchfields had everything going for it - until pupil numbers rose to almost 2,000 by 1966, resulting in a degree of overcrowding. Never short of ideas, the school introduced 'team teaching' as a short-term solution, which was reportedly very successful.

'Buy British' was the message of the annual British Industries Fair at Castle Bromwich. The Fair began in 1920 and grew year by year; after the 1936 show the building was extended to 708,000 square feet, and the following year the Fair was estimated to be five times its original size. The display by West Bromwich manufacturers naturally concentrated on the heavier sections of industry. West Bromwich - also known as the city of 100 trades - has long been regarded as the undisputed centre of the spring trade; in 1951, out of a total of over 90 spring manufacturers, 20 were in West Bromwich, so it is entirely appropriate that this display should feature 'The largest volute spring in England', weighing six hundredweight. Geo Salter, advertised here, has always been one of the most important manufacturers. The firm moved to West Bromwich in 1790, and the sheer quantity of items that has left its workshop since that date defies the imagination. As well as the springs, weighing machine springs, iron forgings and roller bearings advertised here, products include everything from roasting jacks to typewriters. In 1829 Salter's made springs for Geo Stephenson's Rocket, and during WW2 the firm manufactured more than 750,000,000 springs for war purposes.

A *well-handled family business*

The 1920s were to prove an important decade for Thomas George Fuller, of Handsworth. He began it as a police officer at Kenyon Street Police Station, Hockley, Birmingham, and ended it running his own coal haulage business, assisted by a mate, and using horses and carts. At first he worked out of the family home, with facilities at nearby Handsworth Coal Wharf, and as his business grew he moved to Soho Pool Wharf where he received coal deliveries by train direct from the mines; he then bagged the coal for delivery to his customers. Thomas Fuller's venture turned into a profitable little concern, and in due course he was joined by his son Thomas Harry Fuller.

Thomas Harry left school at 14 and worked in the coal business with his father until 1940. He then joined the RAF, and was to be away for nine years. During this period

Donald John Fuller, Thomas George's younger son, joined the firm; he was subsequently called up for National Service, returning after two years. With Thomas Harry back from the RAF, having been mentioned in despatches, the family was once again able to devote its full attention to the business, which had virtually run down during the war years and had to rebuilt. The horses and carts had by this time been replaced by lorries, and another coal round was purchased, covering deliveries in the Kingstanding and Perry Bar areas of Birmingham.

The founder retired from the business in 1953, and subsequently sold the firm to his two sons. However, their partnership came to an abrupt end when Thomas George died suddenly at the age of only 48. His sons Graham Robert and Keith Thomas were aged 20 and 16 respectively, and with the responsibility of supporting their mother and their younger brother and sister, who were both still at school, falling onto their young shoulders, they had no alternative but to assist their uncle Donald John in running the business. Then in 1966, when Donald John wished to withdraw his interest from the business, the brothers bought him out.

It was Graham Robert and Keith Thomas who had to deal with the consequences of the introduction of smokeless zones. Inevitably this led to a decline in the coal trade as

Above left: *Founder Thomas George Fuller.*
Below: *Thomas George Fuller on the left.*

households switched from coal fires to other forms of heating. Naturally, this was very much on the boys' mind; one option which they considered was developing into the transport field, which they were entitled to do as they had an O licence for hauling goods. One day when Graham was out on his coal round he happened to mention to one customer to whom he was delivering coal that smokeless zones would have a major impact on his business and he would like to diversify into the transport industry. The customer replied she had a son-in-law who worked in his father's transport company, and suggested that Graham telephone them as they were always on the look out for sub-contractors. She then gave Graham the telephone number of A G Lowe & Sons Transport, who by coincidence were based in Hockley - Thomas George Fuller's old stamping-ground.

Graham duly contacted A G Lowe, and this was the beginning of a long and successful business association. The very first load which Fuller's carried for Lowe's was a consignment of rubber coils going to Leeds; many more

Above: Thomas Harry Fuller on the left with horses Tommy Boy, Boxer and Goliath. Right: Graham Fuller in the mid-1960s. Bottom: The bus restored to glory by Fuller & Sons for entry into the Vintage Rally scene in 1997.

followed, with Graham taking charge of the transport work while Keith continued with the remaining coal deliveries. Before long Graham had obtained a contract from Jervis Engineering of Minworth to deliver machine parts to JCB at Uttoxeter, and it was clear that the move into transport had been a wise one. By 1969 the coal trade had dwindled away to virtually nothing, so this side of the business was wound up and Keith went over to driving.

With their O licence replaced by a full Transport Operator licence for hauling goods in the UK, Fuller's was set to expand. They already possessed one Ford and one Austin, and in 1970 they purchased a 16 tonne Leyland Comet, which was the first new vehicle bought specifically for transport deliveries, and Graham used this for deliveries in the London, Manchester and Bristol areas. The next additions to the fleet were another 16-tonner and a 30 cwt pick-up for express deliveries. The company was also able to move out of the family home in Church Lane, Handsworth Wood, relocating in 1972 to premises in Everest Close, Smethwick, where they had some 5,000 square feet of warehousing.

In the mid 70s Graham decided to leave the driving to the others, and came off the road to concentrate on managing

the business. The fleet increased steadily; by the early 1980s Fuller & Sons Transport was operating a total of 17 vehicles, and were occupying 5,000 square feet of storage at Halesowen in addition to the original 5,000 square feet in Smethwick. Having become involved in warehousing and

storage, this became an increasingly important aspect of the business, and by 1986 even more space was needed. It was at this point that the company moved to the site at Kelvin Way, West Bromwich, where it is today. This site occupies a total area of 1.1 acres and consists of a single storey office block with an adjoining 10,000 square foot warehouse and a purpose-built workshop.

Fuller & Sons Transport, still co-directed by Graham and Keith, now operate as a Transport Contractor, acting as a groupage and consolidation depot with warehousing and storage facilities. Their main customers are brewers scaffolding manufacturers and suppliers of household goods, and they also act as agents for 16 shipping companies, loading an average of 30-40 containers a week for export all over the world. These containers are moved by other hauliers, and Fuller & Sons has its own general haulage transport fleet of 12 vehicles, the bulk of which are high curtain siders. With a total staff of 25, the company likes to keep local employees, and has developed a reputation as something of a trouble-shooter; it has a dynamic and flexible approach and will bring its expertise to

bear on any problem which customers bring along. All kinds of cargoes are entrusted to their careful handing - even a Formula One racing car. Graham himself is very much a vintage commercial vehicle enthusiast, and has acquired and restored a number of interesting vehicles which can be seen at rallies all around the country.

A family business for almost 80 years and spanning three generations already, Fuller & Sons Transport exists to provide a reliable personal service to its customers and a safe job for its employees. It aims to be both competitive and fair-minded, and remains on friendly terms with other hauliers; and well to the fore amongst its plans for the future are: to make profits and stay happy. So, with the road transport industry is faced by a number of legislative and economic challenges as we go to press, we wish them much happiness and profit in the future. With such a proven track record of expertise and reliability in both haulage and handling, their success is assured.

Top: The Fodaen lorry discovered and refurbished by the company in the early 1990s.
Above left: *Graham and Keith (directors) in 1999.*
Below: *The fleet today.*

Expertise and service to suit every body

The origins of Fred Smith & Sons (Motor Bodies) Limited can be traced right back to the early 1930s, when coachbuilding was a traditional craft requiring a high level of skill and dexterity. Fred Smith was employed as a foreman painter at old established coach-builder W J Smith & Sons until 1932, when he left to set up his own business, together with his sons Stanley and Alec. At their premises in Lyng Lane they offered body building and repair work for both cars and commercial vehicles, as well as coach painting and sign-writing. Fred and Stanley specialised in coach painting and signwriting, while Alec set the office up and took care of the paperwork.

When war broke out some years later, the young company carried out work on a great many War and Ministry vehicles as well as continuing to provide a service to civilian customers - all of which amounted to a very heavy workload; but in the long term the Smith's efforts proved worthwhile, and after the war, with local businesses rebuilding their trade and investing in transport fleets, and more and more families acquiring private cars, their business continued to grow. Tipping lorries became something of a speciality, with firms such

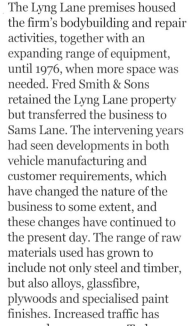

as BP Shenton engaging Smith's to construct the body and paint the vehicle in the company livery.

The Lyng Lane premises housed the firm's bodybuilding and repair activities, together with an expanding range of equipment, until 1976, when more space was needed. Fred Smith & Sons retained the Lyng Lane property but transferred the business to Sams Lane. The intervening years had seen developments in both vehicle manufacturing and customer requirements, which have changed the nature of the business to some extent, and these changes have continued to the present day. The range of raw materials used has grown to include not only steel and timber, but also alloys, glassfibre, plywoods and specialised paint finishes. Increased traffic has made minor accidents an everyday occurrence. Today Fred Smith & Sons are listed by most major insurance companies as an approved vehicle repairer, and the

Above: *Mr Fred Smith (on the right).*
Below: *A new tipping lorry built and painted by the company standing outside Guest Motors New Commercial Vehicle Department in Old Meeting Street.*

private repair shop is equipped with the latest spray booths and computerised paint mixing processor which ensures that paintwork is finished to the highest possible standards.

Technology has also become a vital part of the commercial body repair workshop, where a state-of-the-art alignment system means that damaged chassis and bodywork repairs can be carried out with a very high level of precision and accuracy, while wheel and axles are also aligned by laser. Similarly in the commercial body building workshop the very latest composite and bonding technology is used in the construction of refrigerated bodies.

But although the younger generation of Smiths have more technology at their fingertips, the traditional bodybuilding and signwriting skills have not been lost; and the firm still believes in providing customers with a one-to-one service. The company has built up a loyal workforce of a very high calibre, committed to providing the very best customer care, and including many employees who have been with

the company for 15 years or longer. Again, the company takes advantage of new training schemes and initiatives to ensure that its staff have every opportunity to gain recognised qualifications, but on-the-job training remains of prime importance.

A service which was introduced relatively recently is truck rental. A complete range of vehicles is available, including tractor units, box vans, curtain siders, refrigerated-body vans and trailers, with the option of full maintenance and breakdown cover. Short term hire can be invaluable to customers whose transport needs fluctuate, or to overcome sudden emergencies, while many companies find that contract hire assists budgeting and cash flow. The Truck Rental division has proved a great success, and further expansion is planned for the future. This division recently moved to new premises in Kelvin Way - Fred Smith & Sons fourth site in West Bromwich. The Lyng Lane site has become the company's vehicle testing station and mechanical repairs division; the Commercial Paint Shop is situated in Watton Street, and the premises in Sams Lane is now the company's head office. With not far short of 70 years in the motor trade, Fred Smith & Sons has built up an enviable amount of knowledge and experience, and this, combined with the traditional values of a firm which has been in the same family for four generations, means that no problem is too big for them to handle, or too small for them to care about.

Above left: *New wheeled AEC for Webb Bros Bilston showing old terraces opposite the works being demolished. The picture was taken facing up Lyng Lane.*
Top: *Horse-drawn coach - repainted for the carnival. Standing is Mr Stanley Smith, seated is Mr Alec Smith.*

The family business whose success comes in cans - not can'ts

Major William Hall Keys, born on the Isle of Wight in 1860, was a remarkable man by any standards. As well as founding the successful family firm of W H Keys Ltd he had a distinguished military career, and had many adventures in foreign parts. His travels began at the age of 21. Having grown up in West Bromwich - where he had moved with his family at an early age - he trained as a chemist before becoming a private in the 1st Volunteer Battalion South Staffordshire Regiment in 1880. The following year he went to South Africa to enlist in the Basuto War, but arrived in Queenstown to find the fighting over. Nothing daunted, he took a job in a wagon-maker's shop, and went on to explore South Africa

and Australia. By the time he returned to England in 1885 his experiences included tramping 150 miles from Queenstown to East London (SA) and sleeping on the Veldt, serving in the Military Police as a convict guard, working as shipping clerk, waiter, billiard marker, draughtsman, Zulu trader, on an ostrich farm and as submanager of a sugar estate in Natal, and living as a bushman in Queensland; and he could also claim the distinction of having had charge of several hundred South Sea Island cannibals on a sugar estate on the Pioneer River.

Two years after his return to England, he acquired a piece of land next to the canal in Church Lane and began blending oils and greases. He also set up tar stills to distill tar residue, brought from the gas works by horse-drawn barges. Keys' early products are thought to have included various types of oils and greases for use in paints and disinfectants. He also used large mixers for blending bitumens and manufacturing mastic asphalt and bitumen compounds for road construction, roofing and coatings. Finished materials were packed in wooden

Above left: *Major William Hall Keys.*
Below: *Valley Bridge, Scarborough.*

barrels and taken on the firm's own boats to the Oldbury railway goods yard, to be despatched to customers.

For the next 30 years or so William remained in West Bromwich, building up his business and taking an active role in public life; he was a prominent Freemason, served on the Town Council for 12 years, was a director of West Bromwich Albion between 1896 and 97, and just prior to the outbreak of war raised a troop of Boy Scouts, acting as Scout Master for four years. In 1900 he took a commission in the 1st Volunteer Battalion South Staffordshire Regiment, holding the rank of Captain when the battalion was disbanded in 1908. Then in 1914, at the age of 54, he was appointed recruiting officer at West Bromwich, and subsequently went to France with the 9th South Staffords (Pioneers), leaving the business in the capable hands of his wife. After being wounded three times, including at the Somme, he was finally invalided out of the Army in April 1918.

Following his return from active service Major W.H. Keys remained at the head of the business until his death in 1945. He was succeeded as Managing Director and Chairman by his nephew, Major H.W. Keys who guided the company successfully until 1974. He also followed his own father as Chairman of West Bromwich Albion Football Club from 1947-1963. He was then appointed Club President, a position which he held until his death in 1974.

Over the years the products and processes have changed. With the closure of gas works, supplies of crude tar came to an end and the business now concentrated on bitumen blending and mastic asphalt. These days the company uses bitumen blending tanks, computerised filling systems and oil-fired equipment for heating processes in order to manufacture a wide range of bituminous solutions, compounds and water based coatings. These are used within the building, electrical and pipe manufacturing industries, for roofing, waterproofing, insulating and coating purposes.

W.H. Keys Ltd. is committed to remaining a family business and has now passed to the third generation - through to the current Chairman Michael Keys Mould. Michael Grainger who has served in the Company for 43 years is the current Managing Director having taken over from Brian Keys Statham who died in 1992. With over a century's experience passed down from generation to generation and now complemented by today's technology, the Company is ideally placed to meet all its customers requirements. It offers flexibility and competitiveness backed by a first class U.K. delivery service and a business philosophy that no order is too big or to small to handle. Success, it is always said at W. H. Keys, comes in 'Cans, not Can'ts'.

Above: *Barges transporting barrels.*
Below: *The Annual General Meeting of May 1965.*

Steeling the heart of the Black Country

The iron and steel industries came to the area to the north-west of Birmingham in the early 19th century, and as collieries and ironworks proliferated the area became known as the Black Country. Bromford Mill existed long before this; there is evidence to suggest it may have been a corn mill as far back as the beginning of the 14th century, but certainly by the early 17th century it was a blade mill, grinding sword blades. Throughout the rest of that century and the first part of the next Bromford Mill was adapted at various times, by successive owners, to carry out different processes for the iron and steel industry; and by 1780 it had become a water-powered wire mill owned by Walsall lawyer Roger Holmes. It then came into the hands of two Black Country families who were already established in the iron industry: the Jessons and the Wrights. Expansion began at Bromford Ironworks under this partnership, and continued under the Dawes family who subsequently took the ironworks over and remained in control until 1887. During this period new buildings were erected, new plant installed, and new processes developed, and Bromford became one of the leading wrought ironworks in the Black Country, with an excellent reputation for quality, rolling such products as plating bars (used by edge-tool manufacturers), nail rods, boiler plates, sheets and fancy iron (with patterned

surfaces), and shipping them to many parts of the world. John Dawes & Son acquired their own blast furnaces, which meant that they could make their own pig iron and thus control the quality of the raw material; and later the firm developed its own collieries too, to provide its fuel for the furnaces. Bromford Ironworks enjoyed great success until around 1880, but by that time the iron industry was facing two major problems: local supplies of iron ores were being exhausted, while new steelmaking processes meant that steel was now cheaper than wrought iron. When, on top of all this, a general trade depression set in, the inevitable happened and in 1887 Bromford Ironworks was declared bankrupt.

Within a few months the ironworks had new owners and was reopened as Bromford Iron Company. Oldbury businessman Ezra Hadley died a few years later, leaving the venture to his partner, former Bradford cloth merchant Benjamin Scarf, and the Scarf family were to head the company for more than half a century, with Benjamin's son Fred joining his father and subsequently becoming sole owner before registering the business as a limited company, with himself as managing director, in 1902.

Above: *An early advertisement.*
Bottom: *Staff and employees from the early 1900s.*

The Bromford Iron Company, with its small workforce of around 100, engaged in both wrought iron production and rolling; by 1904 production had ceased, as had the rolling of bars, and the works concentrated on strip. Conversion to a limited company had raised sufficient capital to convert the mill to re-roll steel, and with the new plant installed Bromford became the first continuous rolling mill in the Black Country, producing hot and cold rolled strip for a variety of end users. Following modernisation in 1924 the business began to move towards the production of precision rolled steel strip. By now Bromford Iron, still run by Fred Scarf, had developed into a sufficiently well-established concern to survive the war and the pressures on the steel industry during the 20s and 30s. But Fred Scarf's health was beginning to fail, and when it became clear that the company was heading for a crisis due to the wartime shortage of raw materials, arrangements were made for Darlington & Simpson Rolling Mills to take over the business. Darlington & Simpson ran the mill between 1940 and 1943, then sold it to a local man, Joe Ashmore. When much of the steel industry was nationalised in 1951, to be de-nationalised again two years later, Bromford escaped because it was so small; Joe Ashmore managed to keep the mill going, but it became severely run down.

In 1958 Charles Cooper bought the dilapidated mill; in January 1959 the Bromford Iron & Steel Company Ltd was formed, and an on-going programme of modernisation and expansion got underway which gave the mill a new lease of life and ultimately led to the success which the company enjoys today. As one of the leading producers of hot rolled steel flats and special sections, Bromford Iron & Steel supplies high quality products to end users in all sectors of industry, both at home and abroad, exporting to destinations including Europe, the Middle and Far East, the USA, Australia and New Zealand. Specialising in small runs, Bromford Iron & Steel has the expertise to produce small quantities of tailor-made special products made to customer's specifications. The company became part of Ash & Lacy plc in 1995, and has continued to invest heavily in production equipment and facilities; its modern plant, coupled with its unique fund of experience, assures the high quality of Bromford's products both now and for the future.

Above left: Bromford's mill in 1965.
Top: The yard in the 1930s.
Below: Bromford's modern plant today.

Building confidence

The meeting of William Garland and Michael Fahy was an important event in the history of Anglo Holt Construction. The two men met whilst working for 'Cubitt', a long established company which is now part of 'Tarmac'. Eventually, William and Michael decided to branch out together and establish their own construction company. Therefore, in 1969, Anglo Holt was founded in Tipton.

The company was set up under what was then considered to be a new philosophy -'design and build'. In fact, this way of working was pioneered in Victorian times by the famous builder of the last century, William Cubitt. Anglo Holt became specialists in this method of working which is now accepted as the natural alternative to traditional methods. The customer is given a firm price and can hold just one company responsible for the project which means that the whole process is a lot more clear-cut than the traditional methods of construction. This philosophy, combined with the company's policy of investing all profits back into the business, has enabled Anglo Holt to be built, with teamwork, into the successful business that it is today.

Anglo Holt's first contracts were small ones with top companies such as: Austin Rover; British Gas; Jaguar; GEC and Goodyear Tyres, to name but a few. This initial success meant that after only two years in business the company could move premises. The move took place in 1971 and Anglo Holt relocated to West Bromwich occupying premises located above Lloyds Bank and later the Leicester Building Society. West Bromwich was chosen as the new base for Anglo Holt because of geographical reasons and because of the supply of good, technical people available there. Indeed, the company has been investing in the town and its buildings and people ever since.

The company continued to thrive and in line with their policy of investing profits back into the construction business, Anglo Holt branched out into property development. After completing a small job for Goodyear the company was told that if they wanted to bid for the next job they would have to fund it as it was to be a 'lease back project'. With the support of their bankers and good legal

Above left: William Garland and Michael Fahy, co-founders of the company.
Below: Comet Retail Discount Store with office development.

advice from their solicitors, Anglo Holt put together a package which was subsequently approved. This project, completed in 1972, became Anglo Holt's first property investment in Bloxwich.

Over the following decade Anglo Holt continued to flourish maintaining their policy of design and build. An example of the flexibility of this policy is the Royal Bank of Scotland building in Solihull. In 1986, the company acquired a cinema located in the High Street. Although the property had potential Anglo Holt continued to run it as a cinema because of its importance to the town as a popular entertainment asset. The cinema was run until mid-1990 when the opening of a multi-screen cinema and a film distributors' ban on new films for small cinemas finally killed it off. However, Anglo Holt redeveloped the site and leased it to the Royal Bank of Scotland for 35 years.

In 1990 Anglo Holt took their 'design and build' philosophy to heart and in fact designed and constructed a building of their own! This steel framed building, clad in a quality brickwork outer skin with a pitched tile roof became their Head Office in West Bromwich. The headquarters provide two storey high office accommodation for the building houses management, design and administration teams and also serves as a central meeting point for clients and consultants working with Anglo Holt. The nineties also saw Anglo Holt investing in the latest technology in order to maintain and further their success

in the construction industry. The design office drawing boards were converted to the state of the art Computer Aided Design System securing the comprehensive in-house design capability of the company. Indeed, the company continued its success undertaking many big construction projects and innovative land acquisition projects. Amongst these projects have been the £12 million building constructed for Land Rover; the new centre built on a former landfill site for Ralph Martindale; the building of Drakes Court, the new premises for Hartle Building Mechanical Service; the purchase of Rapida, a prime development site in the West Midlands; the purchase of Bridgeside; and a £7 million contract from Business Post to build new facilities.

From Rover's preferred supplier base of several thousand companies, only around 30 who are deemed to have made the greatest contribution to Rover's business, receive the coveted 'Supplier Excellence Awards'. Anglo Holt were presented with the Bronze award in 1997, followed by the Silver award in 1998, the last year in which the awards were presented from Rover. That, combined with a turnover in excess of £25 million are indicators of the continued success of Anglo Holt, now in its third decade of business serving the whole of the UK, but still firmly based and committed to West Bromwich and its people.

Above left: *Anglo Holt Head Office.*
Top: *The B&Q Superstore at West Bromwich.*
Below: *Today's directors.*

Representing West Bromwich

The year 1910 was important for Adcocks Solicitors. It was in this year that after having served articles to Stephen Gateley of Birmingham, Leonard Hedley Adcock was admitted as a Solicitor. More significantly, this was the year in which he made his next move towards setting himself up in practice. On the 18th of July, Leonard purchased the West Bromwich practice of Duggan and Elton, Solicitors of Birmingham' for the sum of £50 and thus, initiated the life of Adcocks Solicitors as it is known today.

At first, Leonard began practising from his family home at 396 High Street, West Bromwich. However, by 1922 he was able to merge his practice with that of William Bache and Sons where he became a senior partner. The newly merged firm had two offices in the town, one at the original High Street and the other situated at Lombard Street before moving to New Street.

The firm continued to practice successfully over the following years and in 1938 Leonard's son, Hedley John Adcock, joined his father in what could now be called the family business. The advent of the second world war caused a temporary disruption for the practice as Hedley was called away on active service for his country. However, Hedley returned to the business in 1951 and was admitted a Solicitor. Sadly, a year later in 1952 Leonard Hedley Adcock died at his desk

from a sudden heart attack. His son-in-law, J J Williams, married to Leonard's daughter Mary Adcock, was admitted as a Solicitor at about this time. Hedley took the opportunity to part company with 'William Bache and Sons' and he set up practice with J J Williams in 21 High Street as 'Adcock & Williams'. This partnership lasted until 1965 when Hedley transferred to Stone Cross where the business continued until it moved to St Michael Street, its present headquarters.

Another Adcock generation, Mark Hedley, joined in 1974, was admitted a Solicitor in 1986 and is currently the senior partner of the firm. The business expanded over the following years, acquiring four further practices. Mark's son, Hedley John (III), is presently studying law at Cardiff University and Leonard's great nephew, Peter Hedley Whitton, currently works in a practice in Cradley Heath. Adcocks Solicitors act for a wide variety of businesses and local people and hope to continue its loyalty in representing West Bromwich and its people in the future.

Above left: *Standing left to right: HJ Adcock I (who was the Senior Master of the West Bromwich workhouse), LH Adcock. The boy is HJ Adcock II.* ***Above right:*** *Mark Adcock.* ***Below:*** *Back row (extreme right) LH Adcock. First Row: HJ Adcock I (first left), R Hedley Whitton (second left). Seated: Mrs LH Adcock (second from right), Miss Mary B Adcock (standing bottom right) and Mrs Mary C Adcock (extreme right).*

Cast for a central role in industry

When Mr John Herbert Lavender founded his business in Stafford Street, Wednesbury, aluminium was a relatively new material. Mr Lavender, a metallurgist by profession, set up in 1917 as a consultant and specialist in the heat treatment of steel, but within a short time he had started an aluminium sand foundry on the premises. This was an era when the British motorcycle industry was thriving, and the many legendary manufacturers such as Ariel, BSA, Matchless, Norton and Vincent who commanded respect throughout the motorcycling world became customers of J H Lavender. The company also supplied aluminium castings to the makers of small marine engines, and was a supplier to IBM and Black & Decker.

In due course the founder was joined by son Geoffrey and nephew Alan Lavender. The sand foundry continued at Stafford Street until 1970, when it was sold. Production moved to Hall Green Works, built in the early 1930s to house a gravity foundry.

Over the years the company's markets have expanded. The automotive industry remains an important market, with the emphasis on the diesel sector and aluminium castings supplied for vehicle braking systems and engine management systems. Lavender's customer base also encompasses the gas, construction, architecture and general engineering sectors.

The nature of the company's product has changed little since the early days. The properties of aluminium make it an ideal material for castings: it is strong, light, easy to machine, resistant to corrosion and, being a natural material, is fully recyclable. New manufacturing processes have been developed, however; the company introduced pressure die-casting production in the 1950s, and today Lavender & Co employs both processes: the gravity process is well suited to moderate quantities, while the high pressure process is used for moderate to high volumes.

The current Chairman is Dr Andrew Rose, the founder's eldest grandchild. Run by the Lavender family since the day it was founded and backed by a very experienced management team versed in component design, this small private company can offer a rapid response and a personal service. Hall Green Works is already equipped with state-of-the-art monitoring and control equipment and has QS9000 approval, and the company plans to invest in new diecasting plant, machining plant with CNC facilities and real time X-ray plant with computer enhancement - thus ensuring that Lavender & Co's customer base in many sectors of industry throughout the world continues to enjoy the same excellent, responsive service into the next century.

Below: *The 'Chain gang' from the 1930s.*
Bottom: *Staff and employees from the 1910s.*

Preparations for celebrating the coronation of Elizabeth II kept practically the whole of West Bromwich busy for months before the big day.

Acknowledgments

The publishers would like to thank the following people and organisations for their help in the production of this book

Sandwell Community History and Archives Service (0121 558 2561) - Sandwell MBC Maureen Waldron

Thanks are also due to Margaret Wakefield who penned the editorial text and Ann Ramsdale for her copywriting skills